IMAGES
of America

LONG ISLAND
FREEMASONS

On the Cover: This image was captured before the cornerstone laying of a new Masonic lodge for Jephtha No. 494 F. & A.M. in Huntington on August 25, 1904, on the site of the former Thomas Cushing Livery Stable on New York Avenue. R∴W∴ William L. Swan, acting grand master, officiated the ceremony and is surrounded by William H. Stoyle, R∴W∴ Douglas Conklin, W∴ Alvah M. Baylis, E.J. Van Schaick, J.S. Carr, E.P. Holmes, W∴ Charles Henry Walters, E.A. Cooper, F.W. Galow, Joseph R. Jarvis, W∴ Emmet B. Hawkins, and W∴ Edgar P. Bunce (master). (Courtesy of Jephtha No. 494.)

IMAGES of America
LONG ISLAND FREEMASONS

Ronald J. Seifried

ARCADIA
PUBLISHING

Copyright © 2020 by Ronald J. Seifried
ISBN 978-1-4671-0479-1

Published by Arcadia Publishing
Charleston, South Carolina

Library of Congress Control Number: 2019953704

For all general information, please contact Arcadia Publishing:
Telephone 843-853-2070
Fax 843-853-0044
E-mail sales@arcadiapublishing.com
For customer service and orders:
Toll-Free 1-888-313-2665

Visit us on the Internet at www.arcadiapublishing.com

Dedicated to all the archivists, historians, officers, and brothers of Masonic lodges for their tireless volunteer efforts in preserving their lodge artifacts, without whom this project would not be possible.

*In Memory of Brothers Dalton Levy,
W∴ John V. Forster DSA, and V∴W∴ Ed Moritz.*

Thanks to my wife, Anne, and two daughters, Julia and Sophia, for their patience, love, and support.

Contents

Acknowledgments		6
Introduction		7
1.	The East End: Where the Sun First Shines on New York	11
2.	Central Suffolk: What Is Old Is New Again	29
3.	Western Suffolk: Home of the First Long Island Lodge	47
4.	Oyster Bay: Home of a President and a Brother	97
5.	Town of Hempstead: The Birth of Freemasonry in Nassau County	111
6.	North Hempstead: Where the East Egg and West Egg Meet	135
7.	Glen Cove: A Long Island City	145
8.	Concordant Bodies: Further Light in Masonry	151

ACKNOWLEDGMENTS

Nassau and Suffolk Counties have been home to over 80 Masonic lodges and dozens of concordant bodies since the late 18th century. Today, there are 28 active lodges on Long Island, many of which were able to open their archives for this project: of the Nassau Masonic District, Floral Park No. 1016 (FPL), Glen Cove No. 580 (GCL), Lynbrook-Massapequa No. 822 (LML), Matinecock No. 806 (ML), Paumanok–Port Washington No. 855 (PPWL), South Shore–Long Beach No. 1126 (SSLBL), Spartan No. 956 (SL), Stewart Manor–St. Albans No. 56 (SMSAL), Valley Stream No. 1143 (VSL), and Wantagh-Morton No. 63 (WML); of the Suffolk Masonic District, Alcyone No. 695 (ALL), Amityville No. 977 (AML), Babylon No. 793 (BL), Connetquot No. 838 (CL), Jephtha No. 494 (JL), Old Town No. 908 (OTL), Potunk No. 1071 (PL), Riverhead No. 645 (RL), Smithtown No. 1127 (SML), Star of the East No. 843 (SEL), Suffolk No. 60 (SUL), and Wamponamon No. 437 (WL).

Masonic concordant bodies that provided images include Kismet Shrine (KS), Valley of Rockville Centre (VRC), and Truth Triangle No. 31 (TT).

Thanks go to the following historical societies and libraries: Amityville Historical Society (AHS), Village of Babylon Historical & Preservation Society (BHPS), Baldwin Historical Society (BHS), East Hampton Library Long Island Collection (EHL), the Farmingdale-Bethpage Historical Society and the Farmingdale Public Library Digital Photograph Collection (FBHS), Hempstead Public Library (HPL), Huntington Historical Society (HHS), Long Beach Library (LBL), Mineola Historical Society (MHS), New-York Historical Society (NYHS), Northport Historical Society (NHS), Northport–East Northport Public Library (NENPL), Greater Patchogue Historical Society (GPHS), Rockville Centre Public Library (RVCPL), Sag Harbor Historical Society (SHHS), Sayville Historical Society (SHS), and Westbury Memorial Public Library (WMPL).

Special thanks go to the following contributors: Drew MacCullum (DM); John E. Hammond (JEH); Alexandria-Washington Lodge No. 22, A.F. & A.M., Alexandria, Virginia (AWL); Library of Congress (LOC); Nassau County Dept. of Parks, Recreation & Museum, Photo Archives Center (NCPA); Robert R Livingston Masonic Library & Museum (RLML); Sagamore Hill National Historic Site (SAG); Special Collections & University Archives, University of Maryland (UOM); and Steven Zacchia, curator of the Nassau County Police Museum (NCPM). Some images are from the public domain (PD).

Images without courtesy lines were produced by or are in the collection of the author.

Over 50 different organizations assisted in this project, and within each one of these valuable resources, a brother, sister, historian, librarian, or archivist enthusiastically gave their time and access to artifacts that surpassed my expectations. Due to the lack of space, I am regretfully unable to name each one of these important people. These colleagues are the anonymous exemplars to this book, and to them, I sincerely give thanks for their support.

Abbreviations of Masonic titles used in this book include Worshipful Master (W∴), Very Worshipful (V∴W∴), Right Worshipful (R∴W∴), and Most Worshipful (M∴W∴).

INTRODUCTION

One of the things that attracted me so greatly to Masonry, that I hailed the chance of becoming a mason, was that it really did act up to what we, as a government and as a people, are pledged to—of treating each man on his merits as a man. When Brother George Washington went into a lodge of the fraternity, he went into the one place in the United States where he stood below or above his fellows according to their official position in the lodge. He went into the place where the idea of our government was realized as far as it is humanly possible for mankind to realize a lofty idea.

—Theodore Roosevelt to the Grand Lodge of Pennsylvania,
on the sesquicentennial anniversary of the initiation of George Washington,
November 5, 1902

Freemasonry is a worldwide fraternal organization that is a system of morality, veiled in allegory and illustrated by symbols. Formally organized in London, England, in 1717, Freemasonry initiates men from various professional and social backgrounds, well recommended, with a shared belief of a supreme being without prejudice of religious affiliation. A society with secrets, but not a secretive society, Freemasons forbid the discussion of politics or religion in the lodge, creating an atmosphere of harmony and removing any conflictive and divisive nature. Charity has been an important aspect and virtue of Freemasonry since its foundation.

A Masonic lodge (or temple) is where members become brothers through three ceremonial degrees based on the stonemasons' guilds of the Middle Ages. This period of Western history is when operative masons, the builders of the great cathedrals of Europe, admitted speculative masons into their guilds. In time, speculative masons outnumbered the operative masons, and the masons' secrets were passed down to the Freemasons during the Age of Enlightenment.

Several men were instrumental in the building of the Masonic fraternity in the American colonies and the early days of the United States, including Benjamin Franklin, Paul Revere, and Prince Hall. Long Island Freemasonry traces its roots to George Washington, when the commander in chief attended several military Masonic lodge meetings during the Revolution. The first president was initiated to the Masonic degree of entered apprentice at the age of 20 in 1752 in Fredericksburg, Virginia, and continued an active participation in the fraternity until his death in 1799. Brother Washington's Masonic activities include using the Bible from St. John's Lodge No. 1 in New York City for his inauguration in 1789 (with the oath administered by chancellor and grand master of Masons in New York, Robert R. Livingston), and presiding as the "acting master" for the Masonic cornerstone laying ceremony of the US Capitol building on September 18, 1793.

In April 1790, Brother Washington toured Long Island for five days, visiting several towns that would form Masonic lodges over the next several years. On April 23, he dined at the home of the "Widow Blidenberg" in Smithtown, later referred to as Blydenburg's Tavern, the first meeting place of Suffolk Lodge No. 60 seven years later. On April 24, Washington visited the home and paper mill of Henrick Onderdonk in Roslyn, whose daughter Sarah was the wife of David Richard Floyd Jones, charter member and master of Huntington Lodge No. 26 and Morton Lodge No. 63 in Hempstead.

On February 4, 1784, James Gardiner, John L. Hudson, and Joseph Corwin petitioned to form a lodge in Brooklyn with the name Long Island Lodge. No further records exist of this lodge. On September 5, 1787, a group of brothers residing in Jamaica received the charter for Jamaica Lodge from the Grand Lodge of New York. The only recorded activity of Jamaica Lodge was marching in the procession in the anniversary festival of St. John the Baptist in New York on June 24, 1789. By 1793, this lodge had surrendered its charter due to a lack of activity.

The roots of organized Long Island Freemasonry begin with Huntington Lodge No. 26 of Oyster Bay. In 1793, a group of brothers residing in Oyster Bay and Huntington, led by Moses Blachly, petitioned to form a lodge on the north shore of Long Island, which was granted on March 22, 1793, by the Grand Lodge of New York. Huntington Lodge No. 26, Ancient York Masons of Oyster Bay, Queens County, met sporadically until 1806 before finally surrendering its charter in 1818 due to a lack of activity. This lodge's long-lost meetings most likely occurred in the homes of the members and local taverns, including as far north as Lloyd's Neck. There are only 30 known members of this lodge, 16 of whom became charter members of two lodges that meet to this day.

For three years, Huntington Lodge No. 26 was the only active lodge on Long Island, with members traveling from as far as Hempstead in the west and Setauket in the east. The great distances to lodge meetings forced the brothers to utilize the "ride and tie" method of traveling. Hours before a meeting, two brothers would start out, with one on horseback and the other on foot. The horse rider would travel to a predetermined location, tie the horse to a tree, and continue to walk on foot. The walker would reach the rested horse, ride to the next predetermined location, tie the horse to a tree, and continue to walk on foot. This process would continue to the meeting location, giving the two walkers and the one horse needed rest for their long journey. The brothers would attend the lodge meeting, stay overnight nearby, and start out back home the next day with the same ride and tie method.

On December 7, 1796, an application for a warrant for "a lodge in Suffolk county, Long Island, by the name of Suffolk Lodge" was granted by the Grand Lodge of the State of New York. The first meeting was held on March 9, 1797, at the Widow Blydenburgh's in Smithtown, with the installation of officers including the first worshipful master, Moses Blachly, the first past master of Huntington Lodge No. 26. Seven brothers from Huntington Lodge No. 26 and a "Brother Fagen from Ireland" attended this first meeting. Within the first year, 19 candidates were initiated, led by the first applicant, Woodhull Smith.

Six months later, on June 23, 1797, Morton Lodge No. 63 was granted a warrant. Requested by eight members of Huntington Lodge No. 26 residing in Hempstead, the petition stated one of the reasons to form a new lodge was "the distance they live from Said place of Meeting and The fatigue and trouble which an attendance Theron creates." Named after deputy grand master of the Grand Lodge of New York Jacob Morton, this lodge meets to this day as Wantagh-Morton No. 63.

On July 26, 1804, a fourth lodge was formed in the small south fork village of Sag Harbor. Hampton Lodge No. 111 struggled to exist for several years before finally surrendering its charter in 1832. Almost 25 years later, three surviving brothers of Hampton Lodge No. 111, along with brethren from other jurisdictions, formed Wamponamon Lodge No. 437, which continues to meet to this day in Sag Harbor.

In the late 18th century, most brothers were farmers or seamen, professions that may have contributed to the struggles of early Long Island Freemasonry. Due to their work, it was not easy for them to attend meetings or pay regular dues, let alone send representatives to the annual meeting of the Grand Lodge in New York City. The financial strain and traveling difficulties forced Suffolk No. 60 to surrender its charter in 1832 and Morton No. 63 to follow in 1842. Suffolk and Morton were able to reform years later and reactivate their original numbers.

The post-Colonial period of Masonry on Long Island struggled through the anti-Masonic wave of the late 1820s before sentiment toward the fraternity improved and Masonry slowly started to rebuild in the 1850s. At the outbreak of the Civil War, only six lodges met on Long Island. By 1900, a total of 13 lodges were active.

Originally, the Fourth Masonic District consisted of Kings, Queens, (which included Nassau) and Suffolk Counties, putting great strain on the district deputy grand master traveling to each lodge for the annual inspection, as required by the Grand Lodge bylaws. In 1869, Kings county became District Four and Suffolk and Queens Districts were placed in the newly formed District 24. On October 14, 1897, M∴W∴ William A. Sutherland, grand master of New York, designated Nassau and Suffolk as two separate Masonic districts. By the mid-20th century, the former area that covered the entire landmass of Long Island contained eight Masonic districts and 153 lodges.

From Colonial times until the late 19th century, Long Island consisted of Brooklyn, Queens, and Suffolk Counties. In 1898, the western area of Queens County was consolidated as one of the five boroughs of New York City. In the following year, Nassau County was formed, thereby separating the urban areas of Queens and Brooklyn from the suburban Nassau and Suffolk counties. In 1899, Nassau County included the towns of Hempstead, North Hempstead, and Oyster Bay, and the cities of Glen Cove and Long Beach, while Suffolk County included the towns of Huntington, Babylon, Islip, Smithtown, Brookhaven, Riverhead, Southampton, East Hampton, Southold, and Shelter Island.

The early 20th century witnessed financial stability as brothers moved from renting spaces to building and owning their own lodge temples and, in some cases, additional parcels of investment property. When the United States entered World War I in 1917, a total of 17 Masonic lodges were meeting at locations that they could proudly call their own. In the postwar years (1918–1929), 14 new lodges were chartered, bringing the total to 31 lodges throughout Nassau and Suffolk Counties. Society changed drastically with the stock market crash of 1929, and many lodges struggled to maintain their buildings, retain membership, or recruit new members. Between 1929 and 1940, only two new lodges were formed on Long Island, but it is a testament to the dedicated membership of this bleak period that none surrendered their charter.

Masonic membership exploded on Long Island, the birthplace of the modern suburb, in the post–World War II years (1945–1960), when 12 new lodges were formed. Although membership grew steadily in the 1960s, the decade did not see any new lodges, surrender of charters, or mergers between lodges. With dwindling and aging membership, lodges struggled to maintain basic overhead costs and were forced to sell their buildings and rent spaces from other lodges, fraternal organizations, and churches. In the Consolidation Era (1978–present), 36 former Long Island lodges consolidated into 10 lodges that meet today. Across Nassau and Suffolk Counties, 28 lodges continue to meet today.

Despite the membership decrease in some areas, several lodges and concordant bodies have grown at an unprecedented rate, due in part to two or more lodges meeting at one location and interest in the fraternity reaching a wider audience through films and documentaries. Jephtha Lodge No. 494 in Huntington has experienced a 30-percent increase in membership since 2010, with the average age of initiation in the early 40s. The guidelines of the past remain in place, with an extensive vetting process, including interviews and reference checks, enabling Freemasonry to continue its beneficent deeds for the community and society.

The work contained in these pages reflects my personal experience and discoveries and does not represent any Masonic lodge, jurisdiction, or the Grand Lodge of the State of New York. I have been a member of the fraternity for over 17 years and have been very fortunate to meet and associate with hundreds of new acquaintances and friends. Many of these people were instrumental in completing this book. Due to the limited space available, many of these brothers and sisters have been regretfully omitted, and this is my greatest disappointment. I will forever be grateful to these wonderful people who spent time with me completing this project. This book is for all the members of the Masonic family on Long Island.

This portrait of Brother George Washington was painted by William Joseph Williams and given to Alexandria Lodge No. 22 in Virginia, of which Washington was a member. Lodge officers wrote Brother Washington in 1793 that it would be "a source of the most refined gratification the tracing out and contemplating [of] the various ornaments of his character in the resemblance of his person." Williams's portrait shows Washington as a Virginia past master, with Masonic regalia and jewels. Williams did not edit out Washington's smallpox-scarred pockmarked cheeks, the bags under his eyes, the awkward set of his jaw (from numerous dental issues), a scar on his left cheek, and a mole under his right ear. This is a portrait of a vulnerable, battle-hardened warrior who had given 30 years of indispensable and sacrificial service to his country. This portrait is believed to be the most accurate depiction of Washington commissioned in his lifetime. The original pastel-on-paper Masonic portrait of Washington is in the archives of Alexandria-Washington Lodge No. 22 A.F. & A.M., Alexandria, Virginia. (AWL.)

One

THE EAST END

WHERE THE SUN FIRST SHINES ON NEW YORK

On July 26, 1804, a lodge was formed in the whaling village of Sag Harbor. Hampton Lodge No. 111 was the only civic society in the shipping port located on Gardiner's Bay in the early 19th century, first meeting in the attic of a house owned by brother and treasurer Moses Clark on the corner of Division and Union Streets. Within five years, up to 50 well-known local citizens joined the fledging fraternity. The secrecy of this group of men lent a certain level of mystery and respect when the members appeared in public. Schools were dismissed and locals turned out en masse to see the Masons parade.

The lodge, however, was short-lived. Due to commitments to work and family, fraternal activity decreased, and by 1818, the lodge surrendered its charter. It was reinstated in 1821 and finally suspended for good in 1832. Anti-Masonic sentiment of the late 1820s delayed restoration for 25 years. In 1857, several brothers from other jurisdictions, including Connecticut, the newly formed Peconic Lodge No. 349 in Greenport, and four surviving members of Hampton Lodge petitioned to create a new lodge in Sag Harbor. Named after a Native American term meaning "to the eastward" commonly found in local deeds referencing Montauk Point, Wamponamon No. 437 was formed in 1858.

The relationship between the Greenport and Sag Harbor lodges remained strong through the turn of the 20th century. By the end of 1902, a petition was read in Wamponamon to form a new lodge in the Village of East Hampton. Wamponamon Lodge and the Sag Harbor Cornet Band journeyed to the Oddfellows Hall in East Hampton on June 11, 1903, and presented the Star of the East No. 843 officers' aprons, jewels, staffs, and a Bible to the newly chartered lodge. Eleven years later, a charter was granted to a group of brothers looking to form a lodge in Southampton named Old Town No. 908 . Wamponamon once again led the support by presenting the new lodge with a pair of middle chamber pillars. Westhampton would become the final home of a Masonic lodge on the east end with the formation of Potunk No. 1071 in 1926.

Made of fine Italianate brick, the building on the right was first occupied by G.H. Corwin's Drug Store in Greenport. Peconic Lodge No. 349 met in Mechanics Hall on the second floor. Part of the seal of the Order of United American Mechanics can be seen behind the flag. Years later, Greenport's first telephone exchange was in the rear, and in the 1920s, a speakeasy occupied the floor where the Masons once met.

Chartered on June 19, 1855, Peconic No. 349 met every Wednesday evening over the Young & Wiggins store on Main Street until 1889, when it moved above the G.H. Corwin Drug Store. On November 1, 1903, a new Masonic temple was dedicated to the memory of Brother Johnston for his gift of $10,000 for the new temple. The lodge sold the building in 2005 and moved back to Mechanics Hall until 2017, when it moved over 20 miles west to the lodge in Riverhead. Today, Peconic Lodge No. 349 is the oldest lodge in continuous existence in Suffolk County.

Peconic Lodge can be seen to the right of the Queen Anne–style Greenport Auditorium. Constructed in 1894 by Charles H. Corwin and funded by local community leader and woman suffragette Sarah Jackson, the theater held up to 700 patrons until the devastating hurricane of 1938. Since the late 1940s, the theater has been a family-owned furniture store, but most of the original fixtures are intact, including the stage and balcony.

Every Masonic district is represented by a district deputy grand master, representing the grand master of Masons in New York. Since there are far too many lodges within a state for a grand master to visit and review, the jurisdiction is divided into districts, and a district deputy is appointed to make an official annual visit to each lodge within his district. This is a rare look into the lodge room of Peconic No. 347 on November 2, 1966, during the annual district deputy visit. Pictured from left to right are R∴W∴ Charles Ehrenbreg, R∴W∴ Elwood H. Beaver, W∴ Robert Thompson, and Senior Warden Harold Haupt. (RL.)

The first meetings of Wamponamon No. 437 were at the Suffolk Independent Order of Odd Fellows on the west side of Main Street between 1858 and 1869, when the lodge moved into the third story of the Nassau House on the east side of Main Street, with furnishings supplied by longtime treasurer Dr. Frederick Crocker. Destroyed by a fire in 1877, the building was expanded and rebuilt in brick and renamed Hotel Bay View. Wamponamon moved from this location to the First Presbyterian Church in 1883. (RLML.)

The First Presbyterian Church of Sag Harbor was constructed in 1816 using recycled lumber from the congregation's first building, the "Old Barn Church," dating to 1766. When the congregation expanded, the church sold the building to Christ Episcopal Church in 1844. Wamponamon No. 437 purchased the church in 1883 for $1,700. In 1903, the lodge sold the property to Fahys Watch Case Company for $3,500, with a five-year lease to remain on the third floor. The building was moved one block to the corner of Church and Union Streets and was renamed the Atheneum in 1904. (SHHS.)

This aerial view of Sag Harbor shows the steepled two-story Atheneum on the right in its original location. The Atheneum was a 500-seat community lecture hall and theater. Dances, basketball games, stage plays, a basement bowling alley, and Sag Harbor's first movie theater entertained the local community. Wamponamon met on the top floor until 1924, when the building burned down during a benefit dance recital. Today, it is the parking lot for St. Andrew's Church. (SHHS.)

This is the only known interior photograph of the Masons in the Atheneum with over 60 members, including W∴H. Lillywhite (second row center, in the top hat), taken on June 12, 1912. Because of its central location in the community, Wamponamon No. 437 membership boomed during this period, raising between 10 to 20 new brothers annually. (WL.)

Margaret Olivia Slocum Sage was a philanthropist known for her contributions to education and progressive causes. Married to financier and railroad executive Russell Sage, she inherited his estate of almost $70 million without restrictions upon his death in 1906. Sage spent her summers in Sag Harbor, where she commissioned and built the John Jermain Memorial Public Library, named after her grandfather, who fought in the American Revolution. The library was a gift to the residents of Sag Harbor and is located across from her summer home on Main Street. She passed away in 1918, and her home was purchased by Wamponamon Lodge in 1920.

The home was designed and constructed in 1845 for $7,000 by architect Minard LaFever as a residence for whaling ship owner Benjamin Huntting II. After Huntting's death in 1867, his son Benjamin F. Huntting occupied the house until his death in 1887. The home was unoccupied until 1907, when Margaret Olivia Slocum Sage purchased the Greek Revival home with ornate Corinthian columns and carved wooden doors as a summer cottage. Purchased by Wamponamon No. 437 in 1920, the Sag Harbor Whaling and Historical Museum exhibited artifacts on the ground floor starting in 1936. The building and property were deeded to the museum in 1945, and Wamponamon continues to meet on the second floor. The former mansion is now listed in the National Register of Historic Places.

On December 18, 1902, a total of 27 members of Wamponamon No. 437 living in East Hampton petitioned the Sag Harbor–based lodge for a dispensation to establish a new lodge. Star of the East Lodge No. 843 began holding meetings at Oddfellows Hall at 26 Newtown Lane, East Hampton, on March 20, 1903, and remained at this location until 1922. On the left are the farm buildings belonging to Elisha Mulford, whose home stood on what is now the intersection of Barns and Newtown Lanes. Early members of Star of the East Lodge came from a variety of professions, including merchants, carpenters, plumbers, farmers, doctors, painters, insurance agents, butchers, caretakers, ministers, fishermen, jewelers, and architects. The building still stands in the heart of the East Hampton business district. (EHL.)

In 1907, a new high school wing was added to the rear of the East Hampton Union School's original building. When the school was auctioned in 1922, Star of the East No. 838 made the winning bid of $325 for the rear section of the building. This section was moved onto a building on the corner of Fithian Lane and Main Street and modified to accommodate the lodge's purpose. (EHL.)

Moved to the location where the former Clinton Hall had stood, the center of town activities for years, the lodge restored the building with a new pillared front and vestibule. A modern lodge room was constructed on the second floor, a large ballroom was added to the first floor, and a kitchen was installed in the rear of the building. Later, a basement was built under the entire building where four bowling alleys were installed.

Star of the East No. 838 rented the former high school assembly hall on the second floor, while the East Hampton Village Police Department rented one room over the vestibule. The stock market crash in 1929 prevented the lodge from purchasing the remainder of the building, and in the late 1940s, it was sold to the Veterans of Foreign Wars. Several improvements were made, and the lodge continued to use the second floor until 1978.

Star of the East No. 838 met in its building for over 55 years until a fire consumed the rear third in 1978, destroying the kitchen and part of the roof. The building was completely torn down except for the front foyer. The rear portion was rebuilt with only one story, and the building still stands in the heart of the East Hampton business district. (EHL.)

After the fire in 1978, Star of the East No. 838 met in a portable building on Three Mile Harbor Road. When the temporary structure was sold, the lodge moved its meetings to the top floor of the Whaling Museum in Sag Harbor for several years, which was also the meeting site for Wamponamon No. 437. The lodge currently meets in Scoville Hall on the grounds of Amagansett Presbyterian Church. (SEL.)

Established by brothers of Wamponamon No. 437 in Sag Harbor living in Southampton and Hampton Bays, Old Towne Lodge No. 908 received its charter in May 1914. Constructed in the late 19th century, Old Towne co-owned the Main Street Southampton building with the local chapter of the Odd Fellows, Southampton No. 842 IOOF, from 1915 to 1936, when the lodge purchased the building from the Odd Fellows. Old Town No. 908 continues to meet at this location to this day. (OTL.)

Old Towne's lodge building in Southampton went through extensive redesigns over the decades. Starting in the 1920s, the lodge replaced the original exterior siding with a stucco wall material, and the second-floor pent roof with clay pantiles was installed, blocking the original third-floor windows and reducing the second-floor windows from four to three. The three half-moon windows are accessible from the third-floor attic space. Old Town No. 908 is also one of only three Suffolk County Masonic lodges that have first-floor retail spaces.

The interior of the Old Towne Lodge is pictured set up for the Southampton Chapter of the Odd Fellows. The hardwood floor was not carpeted for many years. Today, the window behind the secretary's desk on the right is used as a fire escape. The lodge room retains most of the original design, except for the treasurer's desk on the left, which is now next to the secretary's on the right to make room for a large organ, replacing the original upright piano. (OTL.)

The altar in the center of the lodge room has two symbols engraved onto the sides: the square and compass of the Freemasons and the three-link chain of the Odd Fellows. The altar would be rotated to display the appropriate engraving toward the entrance prior to an evening meeting. Upon the altar rests the Bible, used as a symbol of the Book of Faith. This altar is still used by Old Town No. 908 .

In 1947, the Masons started raising funds for rheumatic fever research as part of the Masonic Foundation for Medical Research. To raise awareness of the fraternity's benevolent institutions, participation in local holiday parades was more commonplace, and Old Town No. 908 regularly appeared at these events displaying their more charitable endeavors. Brothers dressed in their finest Masonic regalia, with doctors, nurses, and even children proudly standing on elaborate floats in front of the local community. Events such as these helped raise awareness of the Masons and increase membership in the postwar years of the 1940s and 1950s, when membership reached an all-time high. (Both, OTL.)

The Junior Order of American Mechanics is a fraternal organization that started in the mid-19th century. Mechanics Hall was constructed on the corner of Sunset Avenue and Mill Road in Westhampton for $7,000 in 1906. The building was an assembly hall and hosted meetings, movies, dances, live theater productions, and briefly, a school after the 1938 hurricane. In 1907, Masonic brothers in the Westhampton area petitioned Grand Lodge to form a lodge. Persuaded to abandon the idea, it was several years before the Oyster Bay Square Club, meeting at Mechanics Hall, helped organize the Westhampton Square Club, initiating 11 members at its first meeting on February 26, 1925. The Westhampton brothers, finding the arduous 11-mile journey to Riverhead Lodge too difficult during the winter months, once again petitioned Grand Lodge, and later in the year, Potunk Lodge was issued warrant No. 1071. All 41 petitioners met on August 13, 1925, and chose the Native American name *Potunk*, meaning "a place where the foot sinks," or a "boggy place," beating out other suggestions including Ketchabonac and Westhampton. The rural atmosphere of the Westhampton lodge permeated their regalia. Potunk No. 1071 is the only known lodge to have its silver-plated jewels made from lawn mower bushings and odd pieces of brass. Potunk No. 1071 met at Mechanics Hall from 1925 to 1968.

Past masters of Potunk No. 1071 stand in the east of the lodge room at Mechanics Hall in 1948. From left to right are W∴ Herman E. Bishop (1926–1927), W∴ Frank D. Gould (1932), W∴ Luther P. Cook (1933), W∴ Frederick R. Jagger (1934), W∴ Jesse E. Weinelbaum (1936), W∴ Wilbur H. Benjamin (1938 and 1945), W∴ Joseph P. Payne (1939 and 1946), W∴ George J. Miller (1941), W∴C. Cornell Raynor (1942), W∴ John C Eckart (1947), and W∴ James J. Belli (1948). (PL.)

These three brothers of Potunk No. 1071 represent a combined total of 90 years in the craft. From left to right are Gustov Herzog, tiler; Elijah Raynor, secretary; and Ernest Bishop, treasurer. Brother Herzog owned a bakery next to Mechanics Hall; Brother Raynor owned E. Raynor Sons, a successful contractor and builder in Westhampton; and Brother Bishop was the town postmaster from 1886 to 1889 and owned a general store on Main Street starting in 1903.

This image shows Masons marching in a parade on the east end. This is one of several public functions that date to the early 19th century. For some in the local community, it is the only opportunity to see members emerge from their lodge buildings dressed in Masonic regalia. Officers of Potunk No. 1017 are dressed in tuxedos, wearing aprons and jewels of their respective positions in the lodge, and led by the district deputy grand master. (PL.)

In 1962, a small group of Potunk brothers started to research the possibility of purchasing a new parcel. The Old Mechanics Hall needed some structural repairs, and parking was limited for the thriving lodge. In 1966, a potential buyer expressed interest in the old hall. In 1965, the Edward Acker Corporation offered property on Montauk Highway and Union Place as a gift, and R∴W∴ Lloyd W. Wilson purchased the property for $1; he was the only district deputy to purchase land for his district.

On December 27, 1968, the new lodge building was dedicated with M∴W∴ Charles F. Gosnell, grand master, and on January 2, 1969, the first official meeting was held in the lodge's new Westhampton home. Potunk No. 1071 continues to meet in this building to this day. (PL.)

M∴W∴ Charles Francis Gosnell, grand master of Masons in New York, is escorted from the newly dedicated lodge building in Westhampton on December 27, 1968. M∴W∴ Gosnell was a state librarian, running the state library in Albany from 1945 to 1962, and director of libraries and professor of library administration at New York University from 1962 to 1974. The former grand master passed away at the Masonic Care Community in Utica, New York, in 1993. (PL.)

Two

Central Suffolk
What Is Old Is New Again

Central Suffolk County is home to both the oldest and newest Masonic lodges on Long Island and has the unique distinction of having a lodge with the lowest number, which was also the last lodge to join the Suffolk Masonic District. Encompassing the towns of Brookhaven, Riverhead, Smithtown, and Islip, central Suffolk was first introduced to Freemasonry in 1796 with the formation of Suffolk Lodge No. 60.

In the early days of Freemasonry, individual lodges were assigned geographical jurisdictions and had to petition the nearest lodge with a formal request to meet in their town. Traveling by foot made it difficult for brothers to attend meetings just a few miles away. As the fraternity grew and more men living in the same vicinity desired to go to lodge without the journeys that could take two days, more lodges started to sprout up in growing communities. Seven brothers living in the Smithtown, Setauket, and Port Jefferson area, tired of traveling to Huntington No. 26 in Lloyd Neck, petitioned their home lodge to form a new Masonic home in 1796. Brothers Moses Blachly, John Floyd, Ellis Carll, Charles Wheeler, John Mills, William W. Gale, and Shadrack Kelly were the charter brothers of Suffolk No. 60, the oldest active Masonic lodge on Long Island.

By 1826, Suffolk stopped holding regular meetings and was not reformed until 1857. Over the next 100 years, seven more lodges were chartered in the towns of Riverhead, Patchogue, Islip, Sayville, Bay Shore, Medford, and Smithtown. In the late 1960s, a "new" lodge moved to Brentwood from the First Manhattan District but did not formally join the Suffolk District until 1999. The Lodge of Antiquity No. 11 was chartered in 1858 and traces its roots to St. John's No. 1, chartered in 1789.

Central Suffolk has the distinction of being the Masonic home to several prominent locals, including Brookhaven town supervisor Claude Neville (namesake of a park in Center Moriches), New York state treasurer Julius Hauser, and Chief Crazy Bull, grandson of the Sioux chief Sitting Bull.

The first meeting of Suffolk Lodge No. 60 was held at the home of William and Richard Blydenburgh at Smithtown on Thursday, March 9, 1797, with members from Huntington Lodge No. 26 in attendance. Brother George Washington dined here on April 23, 1790, during his five-day tour of Long Island. The lodge continued to meet at the house until September 9, 1801, when it met at the home of Brother Phineas Smith in Dix Hills until early 1802. (SUL.)

This is the house of Maj. Jonas Hawkins, now known as the Hawkins-Mount Homestead in Stony Brook, where Suffolk Lodge met several times in 1802. Hawkins was a member of the Culper Spy Ring during the American Revolution and started running a tavern and store here in 1797. The house is pictured after extensive remodeling during the Victorian period and before it was restored to its original design in the 1940s. (SUL.)

Seen here is the Setauket home of Brother Isaac Satterly, where Suffolk No. 60 met briefly in 1803. Satterly was a captain of militia stationed at Sag Harbor during the War of 1812 and owned and operated a mill located at what is now Frank Melville Park in Setauket. For several years, Suffolk No. 60 was a traveling lodge, meeting at several locations in Coram, Setauket, and as far west as Huntington, at the home of Jeffery A. Woodhull. (SUL.)

The residence of Brother Thomas Hallock, constructed in 1725, was also a tavern, town meeting place, and the home of Suffolk No. 60 from 1805 to 1818 and still stands today in Smithtown. In 1819, the lodge moved to the home of Isaac Jayne in Setauket, where it continued to meet for several years. On June 4, 1819, the lodge's number changed from 60 to 57, because lodges with lower numbers that did not surrender their warrants were reorganized to make all the numbers consecutive. Suffolk No. 57 stopped meeting around 1826, and the charter was declared forfeited in 1832. The lodge was reformed as Suffolk No. 401 in 1857. (SUL.)

Suffolk No. 401 met at the Suwassett Lodge No. 422 of Odd Fellows from 1857 to 1861. Afterward, Suffolk met in the Darling Building from 1874 to 1888 and in a building owned by Caleb H. Davis adjoining the Townsend House from 1888 to 1912. After years of formal and informal appeals, Suffolk Lodge was finally able to return to its original No. 60 on July 25, 1876. Pictured is the present location of Suffolk No. 60 as it appeared in 1912 when vacated by the Presbyterian Society. Erected in 1854 by the Setauket Presbyterian Church, the congregation conducted a mission in Port Jefferson here until selling the building to Suffolk No. 60 for $3,500. The new Presbyterian church on the corner of South and Main Streets opposite the Masonic lodge was dedicated on March 3, 1912, and the new home of Suffolk No. 60 held its first meeting on April 4, 1912. (SUL.)

Located at Cedar Hill Cemetery in Port Jefferson is the grave of the first master of the newly reorganized Suffolk No. 401, W∴ Tuttle Dayton. W∴ Dayton sat in the master's chair from 1856 to 1859, and as past master was appointed to represent Suffolk No. 401 at the annual Grand Lodge communication just prior to his death on June 20, 1861. The brothers erected this brown freestone tombstone monument at a cost of $54. Inscribed above the square and compass is, "He Received Light." On the right, the faded inscription reads, "Tuttle Dayton; 1796–1861; Erected by Suffolk Lodge No. 401."

Chief Crazy Bull, grandson of the famous Sioux chief Sitting Bull of the Hunkpapa Lakota tribe, was a member of Suffolk No. 60 and the first Native American to receive the 33rd degree. The Sioux name "Ta-tan-ka-wit-ko" means "Determining Buffalo." Chief Crazy Bull was baptized in the Episcopal faith as William Jacobs and was known as "Big Chief Bill Jacobs" to his brothers. Born on the Crow Creek Reservation in South Dakota and educated in Kansas, Massachusetts, and Yale University, the World War I veteran and national archery champion taught physical education in Lake Grove for several years. (RLML.)

On November 24, 1866, a total of 20 men contributed $260 for the purpose of creating a new lodge, originally named Ocean Lodge, later renamed Riverhead Lodge. Early meetings were held in a small wooden building behind a store owned by Jacob Meyer on what is now Benjamin Place in Riverhead. On December 19, 1871, Riverhead No. 645 moved to new quarters in the recently completed Odd Fellows Hall on the corner of Main Street and Griffing Avenue, as seen here on the right, and remained at this location until 1893.

George H. Skidmore was the fourth brother to be elected master of Riverhead No. 645 and sat in the east for six years. (1872–1873, 1880–1883). Raised in a prominent local family, his father, Luther, was Riverhead town supervisor. But it was W:. Skidmore's reputation as a local architect of devotional buildings and private homes that cemented his legacy. His designs include Westhampton Presbyterian Church, Christ Episcopal Church in Sag Harbor, and St. Mary's Episcopal Church on Shelter Island. (RL.)

On May 2, 1893, Riverhead No. 645 held its first communication in rooms on the third floor of the new Suffolk County National Bank building on Main Street and continued to meet here until mid-1957. The rooms were dedicated by R:.W:. William I. Chalmers, master of Riverhead Lodge for 10 separate terms in the late 19th century; he was later district deputy grand master of the Suffolk District and an ordained minister. The postcard above shows the bank as it appeared in the early 20th century, and the image below from 1948 reveals how much had changed in the downtown area over the 64 years Riverhead Lodge met at this location.

The permanent home for Riverhead Lodge was made possible through a gift of Brother Henry W. Donald and his wife, Pearl, of Hampton Bays. In 1932, the couple donated half of their estate to Riverhead No. 645 and Riverside Chapter No. 399, Order of the Eastern Star, through identically valued gifts, each totaling over $69,000, which were combined to build the Masonic temple on Roanoke Avenue. The Donalds donated the other half of their estate to Mecca Temple, Ancient Arabic Order of the Mystic Shrine of Manhattan, and the Daughters of the American Revolution chapter in Riverhead. The cornerstone-laying ceremony was held on October 9, 1957, with M∴W∴ Nathan Turk, grand master of the state of New York, officiating, assisted by other grand lodge officers and members of Riverhead No. 645. (Both, RL.)

Above is an original sketch drawn by Mrs. Harold Moore in 1958 and used on the lodge's monthly communication for over 30 years. The lodge was erected by the Maystar Corporation, a joint entity with equal shares held by Riverhead No. 645 and Riverside Chapter No. 399 O.E.S. An amount of $135,000 was spent on the construction, furnishings, and equipment. The stairs leading from the basement collation room to the second-floor lodge room were laid out in symbolic three-, five-, and seven-step landings. Riverhead No. 645 was the Masonic home of former Brookhaven town supervisor Claude C. Neville (1929–1935), the namesake of Neville Park in Center Moriches. (Above, RL.)

This is an artist's rendering of the new temple in downtown Patchogue before it was completed for Southside No. 493 in 1904. Chartered in 1860, Southside met at several locations throughout Patchogue, including the Havens Building on Havens Avenue, the Swezey & Newins building on the northwest corner of Main Street and North Ocean Avenue, the Odd Fellows room, the Mills Building, and Fraternity Hall.

This is a postcard from 1907 of Southside No. 493 in Patchogue. Several Masonic organizations met in this building, including Patchogue Commandry No. 65, Knights Templar; Old Glory Chapter No. 622, Order of the Eastern Star; Suwassett Chapter No. 195, Royal Arch Masons; and Ruth Shrine No. 24, Order of the White Shrine of Jerusalem. The building burned down in 1974, and the bank next door purchased the property, razed the building, and constructed drive-up windows and a parking lot. The lodge later leased a building on Oak Street in Patchogue before surrendering its charter in 2004. (GPHS.)

In late 1868, a group of brothers residing in Islip meeting in a large dwelling on Oakwood Avenue in Bay Shore informed several lodges, including Suffolk No. 60, Peconic No. 394, Wamponamon No. 437, Southside No. 493, Jephtha No. 494, and Riverhead No. 645, of their desire to form a new lodge in Islip. Consisting mostly of brothers from Southside No. 493 in Patchogue, Meridian Lodge No. 691 was instituted on July 22, 1869. Meridian first met in a room over a pickle factory on Grant Avenue for an annual rent of $75 before moving into the top floor of Islip Union Hall on Main Street and Union Avenue from 1884 to 1916. A committee was formed in 1907 for the purchase of a suitable site to erect a permanent meeting place. In 1910, a lot was purchased on the corner of Main Street and Willow Avenue in Islip for $2,800. In 1915, Meridian contracted with Brother Benjamin S. Raynor to erect a new building for $12,982. The building was dedicated on June 1, 1916. Meridian sold the building to residential developers and moved to the Lodge of Antiquity in Brentwood in 2017. The photograph below shows the officer's line for Meridian No. 691 in front of the master's station sometime in the 1920s. (Below, RLML.)

The name of Connetquot No. 838 was unanimously adopted in 1902. Named after a tribe of Native Americans who roamed over the jurisdictional boundaries of the Sayville lodge, the original patent in this eastern part of Islip was made from the purchase from "Winnequaheagh, Sachem of Connetquot," in 1683. Connetquot met on the third floor in the Odd Fellows building from 1902 to 1917, as seen on the right. Originally built as the Gillette Building in 1884, it was more commonly known as the Grand Central Building until its demolition in 1927.

One of the founding members of Connetquot No. 838 and the first junior warden was the proprietor of Sayville's Bakery, Julius Hauser. Starting in 1902, Brother Hauser held several political positions, including chairman of the Democratic Committee of Suffolk County, Islip town clerk, and supervisor of the Town of Islip, and was elected state treasurer in 1907. W∴ Houser was master of Connetquot No. 838 in 1905. (LOC.)

Connetquot No. 838 formed a building committee in 1910, reviewing several sites throughout Sayville. In September 1912, Margaret Brush donated a building site on Gillette Avenue to Connetquot in memory of her late husband, Dr. George R. Brush, a surgeon for the US Navy during the Civil War and a Mason. She also donated several Masonic books belonging to her late husband to the lodge in 1910. On April 1, 1918, Brother Charles R. Brown (raised 1912), Margaret's cousin, donated the old Methodist church on Main Street to Connetquot on the condition the lodge would return the Gillette Avenue property to the Brush estate. (SHS.)

The church was erected in 1848 when Margaret Brush's father, Capt. Jacob Smith, was on its building committee and one of the trustees. Margaret inherited the church and later bequeathed it to her cousin Charles Brown. Brown informed the brothers that he wished all credit for the donation of the church property go to his cousin Margaret. By the time Connetquot moved into the old church in 1918, the building had been unoccupied for 25 years.

The Smithtown Township Square Club No. 946 was organized in Kings Park in 1939. In 1947, a total of 22 members presented a petition to form a lodge, which was granted on June 25, 1948. The first meeting under dispensation was held in Northport on October 15, 1948, and when M∴W∴ Charles W. Frossel, past grand master, presented the charter and instituted Smithtown No. 1127 on June 10, 1949, a total of 77 members were affiliated with the lodge. The lodge purchased property on River Road near the intersection of North Country Road and East Main Street in Smithtown in November 1949. (SML.)

Smithtown No. 1127 broke ground for its new lodge on November 8, 1951, and the first meeting was held there on September 10, 1952. The cost of the building exceeded $40,000. The official dedication did not take place for another two years, with M∴W∴ Raymond C. Ellis, grand master of Masons in New York, presiding. By 1960, membership grew to 255, and several concordant bodies met in Smithtown, including the Eastern Star, the Amaranth, Royal Arch, Council DeMolay, and Triangle. (SML.)

The official dedication of the Smithtown lodge building was held on October 22, 1954, with several officers of the Grand Line present. Because of the large gathering, the ceremony took place outside the building on the unpaved parking lot, with folding chairs substituting for the lodge furniture. Smithtown's first master was R∴W∴ Harry Beckman, president of the Smithtown Square Club, who worked tirelessly for several years to help bring Freemasonry back to Smithtown. (SML.)

This is a view of the east of the public ceremony dedicating Smithtown lodge in 1954 and what appears to be a Packard parked just past the master's station. Despite the formal gathering, a dedication of a lodge is a public ceremony, open to family, friends, and local dignitaries. Today, the Smithtown lodge building hosts two lodges: Smithtown No. 1127 and Dongan Patent No. 1134. (SML.)

Col. Thomas Dongan (1634–1715) was the second Earl of Limerick, a member of the Irish parliament, and governor of the Province of New York. Dongan executed several land grants on eastern Long Island, called the Dongan Patents, in the 1680s. One of these patents was issued to the Commonality of the Town of Brookhaven in 1686. For the first time, the Dongan Patent gave people the right to govern themselves as a corporate body with vast and municipal rights and powers that exist to this day. This unsigned oil-on-canvas portrait came from the Manor of Castletown, Staten Island, which was built for Governor Dongan in 1688. The painting was a gift of Frederic De Peyster to the New York Historical Society. In 1948, a group of brothers meeting in Medford Station created the Dongan Patent Square Club, with intentions to form a lodge. In 1951, Dongan Patent No. 1134 became the last new lodge to be chartered for the Suffolk Masonic District. Although the land on Horseblock Road just east of North Ocean Avenue in Medford Station was donated to the lodge by Brother George R. Holms, Dongan Patent has never owned its own building. Meeting at various locations over the years, Dongan Patent No. 1134 has made Smithtown Lodge its home for the past several years. (NYHS.)

The concept of a lodge at Bay Shore arose in the minds of a group of Masons residing in Bay Shore and Brightwaters who were members of several different established lodges. The Sunrise Square Club met in the Robbins Building on the south side of Main Street in Bay Shore when in 1923, plans were made to form a local lodge. On April 25, 1925, Bay Shore No. 1043 received its charter. The total number of original members under dispensation was 100, but due to the death of Brother William H. Bishop on March 23, 1925, in a seagrass fire before the lodge received its charter, Bay Shore No. 1043's charter membership was reduced to 99. For many years, meetings were held in the Bohack Building on Fifth Avenue in Bay Shore before the lodge constructed a new building on the corner of Union Boulevard and Lanier Lane in Bay Shore in 1952. It was designed by architect Brother Eugene S. Helbig, who followed up this project with the design of the Islip Public Library in 1954. Bay Shore No. 1043 sold the building to a non-denominational church and moved to the Masonic lodge in Brentwood, where it later merged with the Lodge of Antiquity No. 11 in 2011.

The Lodge of Antiquity No. 11 traces its roots to 1849, when St. John's No. 1 joined Phillips Grand Lodge, led by Deputy Grand Master Isaac Phillips during a brief period when there were two grand lodges operating in New York (1849–1858). In 1851, some members of St. John's No. 1 accepted an invitation to return to the Willard Grand Lodge and continued as St. John's No. 1, retaining their original charter dating to 1789. For seven confusing years, there were two lodges named St. John's No. 1. The disaffected body of the Phillips group resolved their differences and returned to the present grand lodge in 1858. After the two grand lodges merged, the original St. John's retained No. 1, and the new lodge was renamed the Lodge of Antiquity No. 11, issued the lowest vacant number available at the time. Antiquity continued to meet at the Grand Lodge in New York City as part of the First Manhattan District for over 100 years. In 1967, Antiquity moved into the cellar of the late-19th-century Brentwood Presbyterian Church at 1900 Brentwood Road, later purchasing the building in 1973. Since the move to Brentwood, the Lodge of Antiquity No. 11 consolidated with Ocean Lodge No. 156, Howard and Prince of Orange Lodge No. 16, Concord Lodge No. 50, Montgomery Lodge No. 68, and Bay Shore Lodge No. 1043. The Lodge of Antiquity No. 11 officially joined the Suffolk Masonic District in 1999, over 30 years after moving to Suffolk County.

Three

WESTERN SUFFOLK

HOME OF THE FIRST LONG ISLAND LODGE

The first Masonic lodge on Long Island was Huntington Lodge No. 26 of Oyster Bay. Chartered in 1793, the original petition states the lodge was "to be formed in the town of Oyster Bay in Queens County, or in the town of Huntington in Suffolk County optional with the presiding officers and brethren on Long Island in this state which lodge shall be distinguished by the name or stile of Huntington Lodge No. 26." Typically, 18th-century lodge meetings were held in taverns, with food and spirits prepared for the brothers gathered around a long table. Dues were owed at each meeting, whether a brother was present or not. Huntington No. 26 had only 30 known members throughout its brief history, more than half of whom later started lodges in Port Jefferson and Hempstead, both still active to this day. Because there was no central meeting place and travel was difficult, Huntington No. 26 only sporadically met until 1806 before finally surrendering its charter in 1818.

Western Suffolk was Masonically dark until 1859, when several brothers began discussions to petition the Grand Lodge to form a new lodge in Huntington. In 1860, Jephtha No. 494 received its charter, with founding members from Joppa No. 201, Charter Oak No. 249, Lexington No. 310, and Suffolk No. 401. Most of the new brothers of Jephtha in the busy seaport of Huntington were seamen, yeomen, ship's carpenters, captains, and sailmakers.

Brothers from Jephtha No. 494 residing in neighboring towns went on to form other Masonic lodges. Alcyone No. 695 in Northport was chartered in 1869 and Babylon No. 793 in 1887, then in an area formerly known as Huntington South. A local Mason was instrumental in separating the Towns of Huntington and Babylon in 1872. Brothers from Babylon No. 793 later formed Amityville No. 977 in 1920, rounding out all four Masonic lodges in western Suffolk county.

At right is the grocery and confectionery store of John Fleet, also known as "Candy John," at the corner of New and Main Streets in Huntington. Jephtha Lodge No. 494 convened for the first time on January 28, 1860, in a room on the second floor and remained at this location until 1885. Charter Oak Lodge No. 249 in New York City donated the necessary Masonic regalia for the officers. (HHS.)

Jesse Carll was a founding member and the second worshipful master of Jephtha No. 494 (1861). A master shipbuilder, he and his brother David were the sons of a retail businessman in Northport. When the senior Carll died prematurely, the sons were forced to survive in the rural areas of the north shore. The brothers first worked in a shipyard in Port Jefferson, and after years of learning the craft and business, opened their own yard with only $400. (HHS.)

On the left is Jephtha No. 494 founding member, first junior warden, and brother No. 6 John Hewlett Jarvis. Jarvis's occupation was yeoman, and he was originally a member of Lexington Lodge No. 310 on Court and Montague Streets in Brooklyn. Brother Jarvis eventually moved to Brooklyn and was dropped from Jephtha's membership on March 27, 1871. On the right is his brother Thomas Woodhull Jarvis in an ambrotype photograph from September 1863. (JEH.)

Located in Melville Cemetery on Sweet Hallow Road is the family plot of the Jarvis family. Brothers John and Thomas are interred near each other, but it is Thomas's headstone that is marked with a Masonic square and compass. The 54th brother to join out of 59 in Jephtha's first two years, Thomas was a baggage master, a person who confirmed that a company received a delivery. He passed away on December 8, 1863, at the age of 23 while stationed with the Union army in Brooklyn.

In 1885, Jephtha No. 494 moved to the third floor over O.S. Sammis & Company Dry Goods Emporium on the northwest corner of Main Street and New York Avenue in Huntington, which they rented until 1905. O.S. Sammis sat on the board of directors of the Bank of Huntington along with several Jephtha brothers, including past masters Jesse Carll, Douglass Conklin, and Joseph Irwin. Constructed in 1884, the building still stands today as a retail space. (HHS.)

In 1869, Jephtha No. 494 purchased a plot of land for $1,000 on New York Avenue just a short walking distance from the O.S. Sammis building. For the next 35 years, the lodge leased the property for $50 annually, with plans to erect a building when funds were available for construction. On August 25, 1904, several Jephtha brothers participated in a cornerstone laying ceremony complete with a time capsule. By March 1905, the lodge building was complete. (JL.)

Completed in 1905, Jephtha No. 494's third and present home was designed not only as a meeting place, but as an income source to subsidize the overhead for the building. The first floor was reserved for two separate retail storefronts, and the second was primarily used as office space. Today, the second floor is used as a private coalition, lounge, and game rooms for the membership. The third floor houses the lodge room and an early dining area and kitchen. The original third-floor dining and kitchen sections were dismantled in the mid-20th century and relocated to the second floor. (HHS.)

The Jephtha No. 494 lodge room on the third floor retains the same layout today, including the officer's chairs, altar, and the "G" symbol above the master's chair. Just above the wainscoting around the lodge room are hand-painted Masonic symbols. In the early 1990s, the ceiling collapsed, destroying the tin tiles and fixtures. The ceiling was upgraded, and new sheetrock walls were added over the original hand-painted Masonic symbols. (JL.)

The Huntington Post Office is on the right in one of the first-floor retail spaces in Jephtha No. 494, which it rented from 1905 to 1925. Huntington postmaster Capt. Emmitt B. Hawkins was Jephtha's master for six years (1895–1898 and 1909–1910). Affectionately known as "Cappy" to his brothers, Hawkins began his term as postmaster in 1897 with an annual salary of $2,000, the highest-paid political position in Huntington. Also a former town supervisor, Hawkins owned three schooners shipping hay and straw between Huntington and the Harlem markets for many years. On the left is the real estate office of Samuel Sweet. (HHS.)

Jephtha No. 494 is seen here from the north. The third-floor cast-iron balcony was used for decorative purposes only and was removed in the mid-20th century. Today, the rust outline of the old balcony can be seen on the front brick façade between the second and third floors. The two half-moon windows above the third-floor second and ninth windows were always blocked from the inside. (HHS.)

On June 2, 1922, a delegation of 12 past masters and 22 brothers from Jephtha No. 494 sailed to Block Island to meet up with Atlantic No. 31 F. & A.M. of Rhode Island for the conferral of the third degree. The historic event was arranged by R∴W∴ Ambrose Rose, district deputy and past master of Jephtha, and his nephew W∴ Lester Littlefield, master of Atlantic No. 31. The six-hour voyage between Plum and Block Islands was made on the ship *Isaac Sherwood*, piloted by W∴ Emmett B. "Cappy" Hawkins, past master of Jephtha. Some of the brothers are pictured here in front of Rose's Hotel on Block Island. (JL.)

On May 27, 1935, Jephtha No. 494 celebrated its 75th anniversary by reuniting several past masters. From left to right are (first row) W∴ John Deans, W∴ Henry Murphy (1924), R∴W∴ Douglass Conklin (1886–1887, 1899), W∴ Charles Walters (1900–1901), W∴ Paul Schaeffer (1930), and R∴W∴ Clifton Gardner (1921); (second row) R∴W∴ Russel Sammis (1927), R∴W∴ Ambrose Rose (1919), R∴W∴ Carrol Welch (1925), W∴ H. Chris Lorck (1932), and W∴ John Boyle Jr. (1931); (third row) W∴ Rudolf Eckel, R∴W∴ Kurt Galow (1923), W∴ F. W. Hunninghouse (1926), W∴ Francis Kane (1935), Joseph Perry (1934), Alvah Baylis (1902–1903, 1908), and R∴W∴ Lawrence Newton (1915). (JL.)

On September 17, 1931, New York governor Franklin D. Roosevelt was invited by Jephtha No. 494 to deliver a speech on the anniversary of the adoption of the US Constitution. Jephtha No. 494 held a special communication—its 1,467th, at Old First Presbyterian Church. Behind the pulpit, from left to right, are W∴ John Boyle, master of Jephtha Lodge; Governor Roosevelt; M∴W∴ Charles A. Johnson, grand master of Masons in New York; and R∴W∴ Guernsey T. Cross, Roosevelt's personal secretary. (JL.)

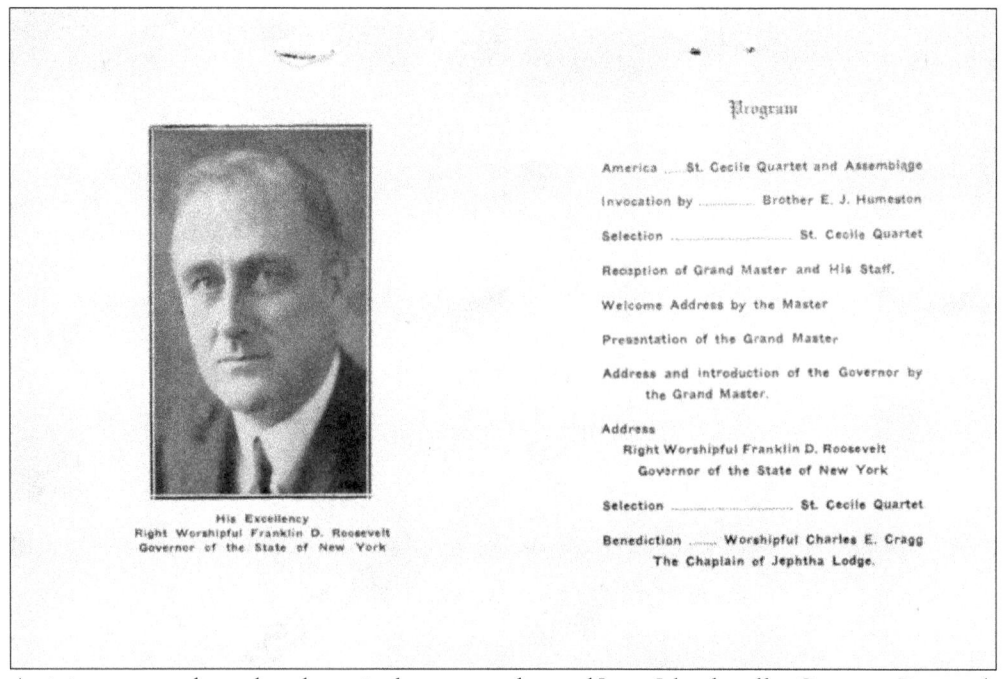

Arriving over two hours late due to inclement weather and Long Island traffic, Governor Roosevelt quipped that the island should be renamed "Longer Island." He was escorted to the pulpit without the aid of a wheelchair, despite the brothers constructing a temporary ramp to the left of the pulpit. Roosevelt was escorted up the ramp by R∴W∴ Douglass Conklin of Jephtha No. 494, receiving a standing ovation from the estimated 350 brothers in attendance, including members from as far as Greenport and East Hampton. (JL.)

Because of the anticipated large audience for Gov. Franklin D. Roosevelt's visit to Jephtha No. 494 in 1931, Old First Presbyterian Church was selected as the logical meeting place, half a mile from the lodge building. The building was the third Presbyterian church in Huntington. The first church was constructed in 1665 on the corner of Spring and Main Streets, but was torn down due to the growing congregation. The second church was erected on the present site in 1715 but was destroyed by British troops for timber used in the construction of fortifications at the Old Burying Ground when occupying Huntington in 1782. The bell, dating to 1715, was commandeered by the British and used on warships. The damaged bell was recovered in 1783 and recast. It was in constant use from 1789 to the 1960s. The present church was built on the same spot in 1784. (Above, HHS; below, JL.)

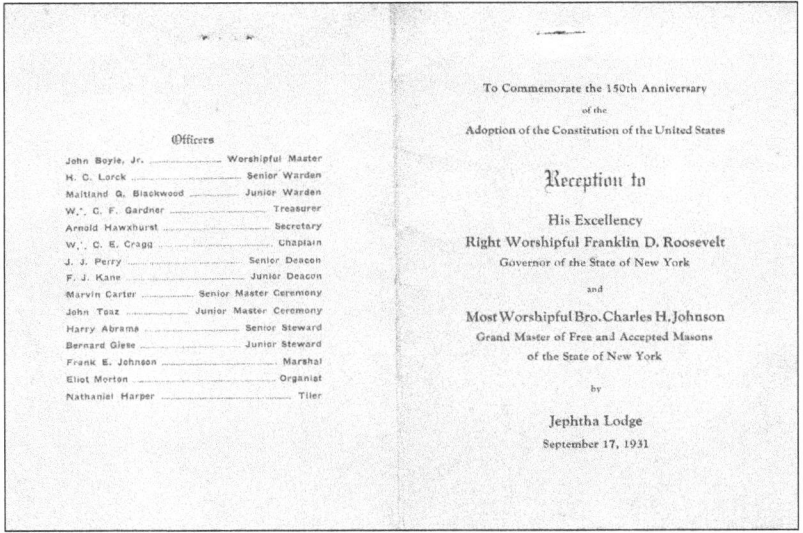

In 1867, a total of 20 brothers from Jephtha No. 494 residing in Northport and Commack petitioned the Grand Lodge to form a lodge in Northport Village. M∴W∴ James Gibson, grand master of Masons in New York, insisted on selecting a name with Masonic significance instead of a town or county. Alcyone and Aquila were the last two names up for a vote by the brothers from a list of recommendations provided by the grand master. Eight slips of paper, seven of which listed Aquila, were placed in a hat. Brother William Sammis, soon to be elected the lodge's first master, pulled the only Alcyone out of the hat. On March 5, 1869, Alcyone No. 695 met for the first time in Northport. Within six years, Alcyone No. 695 moved into a new building constructed in 1875 by Benjamin T. Robbins, meeting for the first time on November 16, 1875. Alcyone No. 695 held meetings on the third floor for the next century and a half. The third door from the left is the original entrance to Alcyone Lodge and the same entrance used today. Soon after Robbins passed away, Alcyone purchased the building in 1916. (ALL.)

A cornerstone on the outside of the Northport lodge is dated 1923, the year the building went through extensive renovations that more closely resemble the façade seen today. This construction project proved to be a disastrous venture after the stock market crash of 1929, putting severe financial strains on the lodge. Alcyone No. 695 was unable to address its overhead costs due to the lack of membership dues collected and vacancy of the first-floor retail spaces, forcing the building into foreclosure by 1937. (NENPL.)

Combining efforts with the Adah Chapter O.E.S. and Asharoken Chapter, Royal Arch Masons, the organizations were able to secure a lease at $500 annually and remain in the building. In 1946, five brothers of Alcyone No. 695 organized the Northport Holding Company to repurchase the property and sell it back to the lodge at cost. By 1953, the new mortgage was paid. Alcyone No. 695 has been meeting in the same building since 1875, making it the oldest Masonic lodge building in continuous active use in both Suffolk and Nassau Masonic districts. (NHS.)

Between 1887 and 1891, Babylon No. 793 started meeting on the third floor of the Willetts Building, the three-story structure in the distance. Located on the southeast corner of Main Street and Fire Island Avenue in Babylon Village, the first floor was occupied by the Dowden Brothers General Store since 1876, with offices on the second floor. Babylon No. 793 leased the upper floor of a new building on the north side of Main Street between Norton & Siegel Inc. and the Babylon National Bank & Trust Company from 1891 to 1910 for $200 per year. (BHPS.)

Founding member and Babylon Lodge's second master, Henry Livingston, was the proprietor and editor of the town's first newspaper, the *Suffolk Democrat*, in the late 1850s. He was a direct descendant of Edward Livingston, author of the Louisiana code and Philip Livingston, one of the signers of the Declaration of Independence. In 1869, Livingston founded the *South Side Signal*, a popular local newspaper instrumental in garnering public support (through Livingston's editorials) for formally breaking from its northern neighbor and incorporating Babylon as a separate town. Because of these efforts, Babylon was never again referred to as Huntington South. (BL.)

In March 1910, Babylon No. 793 purchased Halcyon Hall on Deer Park Avenue for $6,000. Halcyon Hall was used by owner James H. Arnold as a feed store, while the upper hall was rented for dances, entertainment, political rallies, and vaudeville shows and was the former headquarters for the *South Side Signal*. The first communication in the new lodge room was held on September 28, 1910, with Grand Master M∴W∴ Robert Judson Kenworthy and his staff attending the dedication ceremonies. This photograph was taken on April 9, 1947. The lodge remained here until the new building was completed in 1958. (BL.)

The Babylon No. 793 officers line of 1946, led by W∴ William R. Gaggin, is seen in the east of the lodge room in Halcyon Hall. In 1946, late brother Elbert C. Livingston bequeathed $5,000 for reducing the lodge's debts, retiring all bonds for remodeling, dating to 1927. Brother Livingston also donated various jewels and awards that were presented to him by his father, Henry Livingston. The following year, Babylon No. 793 celebrated its 60th anniversary. (BL.)

This is an undated photograph of the Babylon Lodge degree team. Part of a brother's introduction into Freemasonry includes a drama representing the building of King Solomon's temple, with chief architect Hiram Abiff as the central character, murdered for not revealing the secret word of a master mason. Masonic buildings, where lodges and their members meet, are sometimes called "temples," an allegorical reference to King Solomon's temple. (BL.)

W∴ William R. Luchtenberg, master of Babylon No. 793, is pictured in 1976 wearing a tricorn hat. In 1976, M∴W∴ Albert W. Schneider, grand master of Masons in New York, appointed a bicentennial committee to develop a specially designed tricorn hat in commemoration of the 200th anniversary of the signing of the Declaration of Independence. Masters of lodge throughout the state were asked to wear this colonial headpiece in true bicentennial fashion in place of the customary top hat masters wore in lodge communications. (RLML.)

In 1951, Babylon mayor Erastus H. Munson donated 100 feet of frontage on Montauk Highway to Babylon No. 793. By 1953, Halcyon Hall was sold for $30,000, and an additional 70-by-140-foot plot adjacent to the donated parcel was purchased by Babylon No. 793. An 80-by-156-foot parcel south of the temple was purchased from Munson in 1957. The contract to build the new temple was awarded to Brother Arthur W. Anderson in 1957 for $103,444. After a temporary residency at the Odd Fellows Hall on Deer Park Avenue from 1955 to 1958, the lodge held cornerstone-laying and dedication ceremonies on September 10, 1958, with Grand Master M∴W∴ H. Lloyd Jones presiding. Julia Livingston, daughter of founding member Henry Livingston, bequeathed $50,000 to Babylon No. 793 in 1962, which paid off the lodge mortgage. Babylon Lodge No. 793 continues to hold regular meetings at this location to this day.

Obtaining jurisdiction consent from Babylon, Jephtha, and Spartan lodges, the first communication of Amityville No. 977 was held at the Fraternity Hall on Greene Street on November 16, 1920, with a collation following in the Parish House of Saint Mary's Episcopal Church. Most of the 50 founding members were from Babylon No. 793, including the first master, W:. Arthur Wells. In 1922, Amityville No. 977 purchased land on the north side of Avon Place near Broadway from the trustees of Saint Mary's.

The plot of land at Avon Place just east of Main Street, measuring 100 by 127 feet, was acquired on May 16, 1922, by Amityville No. 977. Plans for the new temple were submitted by Max I. Waeber, and construction started soon after. On May 15, 1923, 185 brothers attended Amityville No. 977 for the first time at their Avon Place location. Amityville lodge continues to meet at this location.

Seen here is a still from the 1934 "Our Gang" short *Mama's Little Pirates*, featuring George "Spanky" McFarland, Scotty Beckett, Matthew "Stymie" Beard, Marylin Bourne, and future Freemason Jerry Tucker holding the money bag in the rear. Born Jerry Schatz, the young actor appeared in 23 "Our Gang" shorts from 1931 to 1938, *Captain January* with Shirley Temple (1936), and two radio series in the 1940s: *Jones and I* and *Hilltop House*. (UOM.)

Brother Schatz served in the US Navy in World War II and the Korean War, suffering an injury on the USS *Sigsbee* after a Japanese kamikaze attack on April 14, 1945, that caused him to limp for the remainder of his life. The RCA electrical engineer was raised a master Mason at Amityville No. 977 on September 21, 1995, and was a member of Amityville No. 700 O.E.S. with his wife, Myra. Brother Schatz is pictured here with several local brothers; clockwise from Schatz are V∴W∴ Michael Sherwood, R∴W∴ Glenn Rubin, W∴ Howard Austin, R∴W∴ Wesley Powell, DSA, and R∴W∴ Don Marino. (AML.)

The Dedicated Service Award (DSA) Program was established in 1975 and enables lodges to obtain Grand Lodge recognition for brothers who support their lodges and district with their presence, time, and talent by attending meetings and participating in degrees and programs, with or without holding an office. In April 1975, Jephtha No. 494's first DSA recipient was W∴ Frank Nantista, presented by R∴W∴ Robert B. Anderson, district deputy grand master of the Suffolk Masonic District, and W∴ Joseph Scullion, master of Jephtha No. 494. (JL.)

One of only two historical markers on Long Island commemorating Freemasons stands on New York Avenue in front of Jephtha No. 494 in Huntington Village. Over 30 brothers, friends, and family of Jephtha No. 494 and the Organization of Truth Triangle No. 31 joined Huntington town supervisor Chad Lupinacci and Huntington town historian Robert Hughes for the official dedication of the marker on August 16, 2018. (JL.)

A Masonic certificate is a diploma or traveling passport issued by a grand lodge certifying a member is a master Mason in good standing. Pictured is the Ancient York Masons certificate of George Hallock of Suffolk No. 60 dated August 13, 1800. Officer signatures include W:. Rich Floyd, master; Thomas Floyd, senior warden; David Reeve, junior warden; and Solomon Smith, secretary. It was during this period that Suffolk No. 60 met in the Blydenburgh house in Smithtown.

This is the Masonic certificate of David Harrison of Huntington No. 26 of Oyster Bay, dated December 6, 1801. Harrison was one of only 30 known brothers of the first Masonic lodge on Long Island. The officers listed on this certificate are W:. Ruloff Duryea, master; Jacob McCoum, senior warden; David Lake, junior warden; and Isaac van Nostrand, secretary. Issued within a few months of George Hallock's certificate from Suffolk No. 60, this document is an example of an alternative design made for an Ancient York Masons lodge of New York in the early 19th century. (JL.)

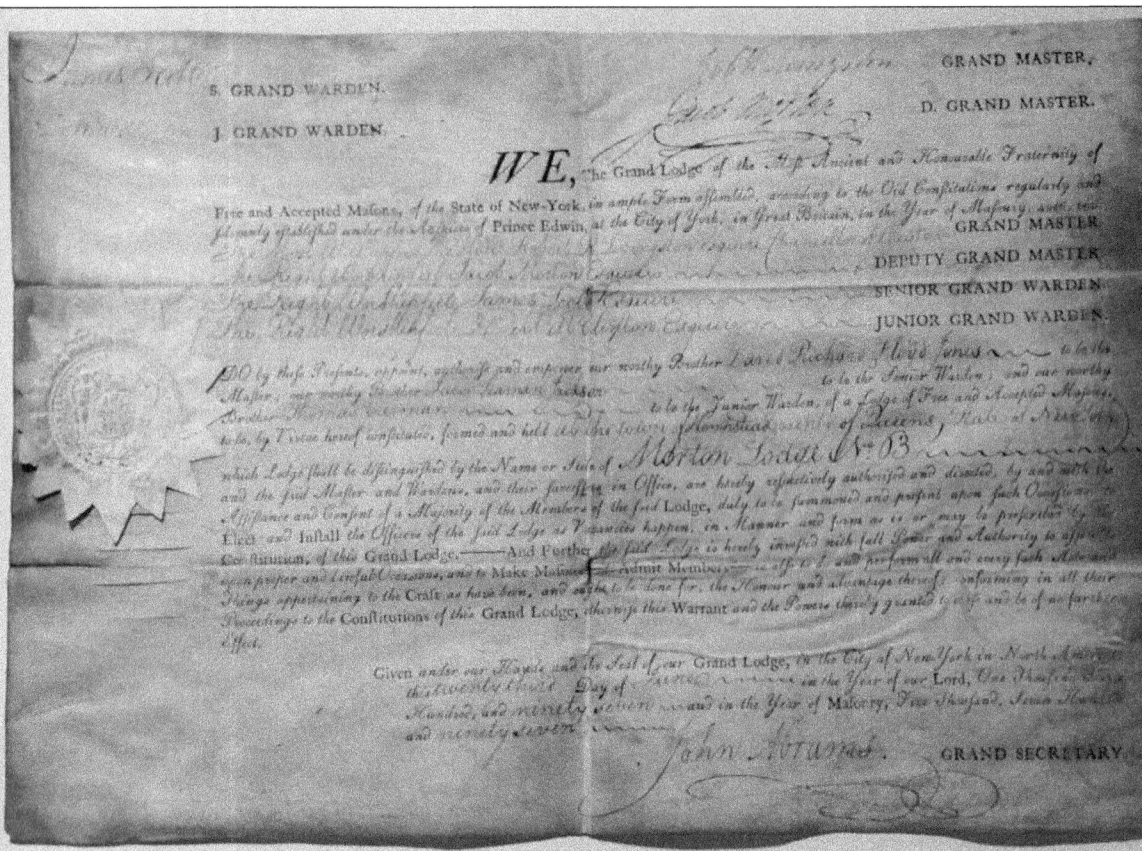

This is the original charter for Morton No. 63 of the "town of Hempstead, County of Queens," dated June 23, 1797. A charter is a document issued by the grand lodge giving authority to Masons to form a lodge. A charter must be displayed at all meetings, placed in the east of the lodge room near the worshipful master, and it is the right of every visiting brother to review the document before meetings to ensure he is not in a clandestine meeting. Signed by John Abrams, grand secretary, this document lists M∴W∴ Robert R. Livingston, grand master; R∴W∴ Jacob Morton, deputy grand master; R∴W∴ James Scots, senior grand warden; and R∴W∴ DeWitt Clinton, junior grand warden and future governor of New York. Morton was grand master of Masons in New York from 1801 to 1805, and Clinton was elected grand master from 1806 to 1819. Morton No. 63's listed officers are W∴ David Richard Floyd Jones, master; Jacob Seaman Jackson, senior warden; and Thomas Carman, junior warden. This delicate document is sealed in an airtight frame and is used only once annually at the lodge's installation of officers and trustees. (WML.)

The original Masonic Bible of Morton No. 63 was presented to the officers and brothers by R∴W∴ Jacob Morton, deputy grand master of Masons in New York. The minutes of the communication held on February 5, 1798, state that "the Worshipful Master presented an elegant Bible from the hand of Deputy Grand Master Jacob Morton, Esq., for the use of the lodge, and requested that it might be entered on the records, as a testimonial of his zeal to the craft and gratitude to this lodge."

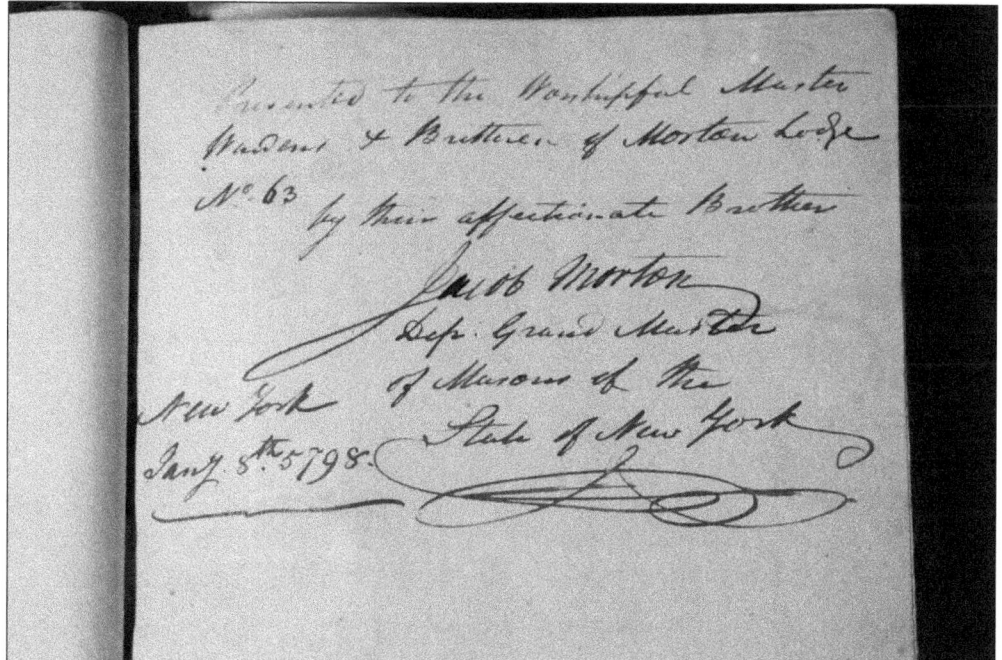

This leather-bound Bible was published in 1793 by John Taylor and is an English translation by Rev. Jean Frederic Ostervald, professor of divinity and one of the ministers of the church at Neufchatel in Switzerland, with 22 illustrations by Abraham Girardet. Wantagh-Morton No. 63 continues to use the delicate artifact once per year for the installation of officers and trustees. Jacob Morton was the master of St. John's No. 1 in New York City who retrieved the Masonic Bible from his lodge at the Old Coffee House on the corner of Water and Wall Streets for the presidential inauguration of Brother George Washington in 1789. (WML.)

Donated to Glen Cove No. 580 on January 19, 1928, this Masonic apron was purported to be worn by Brother George Washington. The apron was given to William L. Hicks by his aunt Catherine A. Mott, the daughter of Leonard and Hannah (Willis) Mott of Sands Point, New York. Hannah Willis-Mott was the daughter of Cornwall and Elizabeth (Hicks) Mott, to whom the apron was given by James Cornwall, a merchant from New York City. (GCL.)

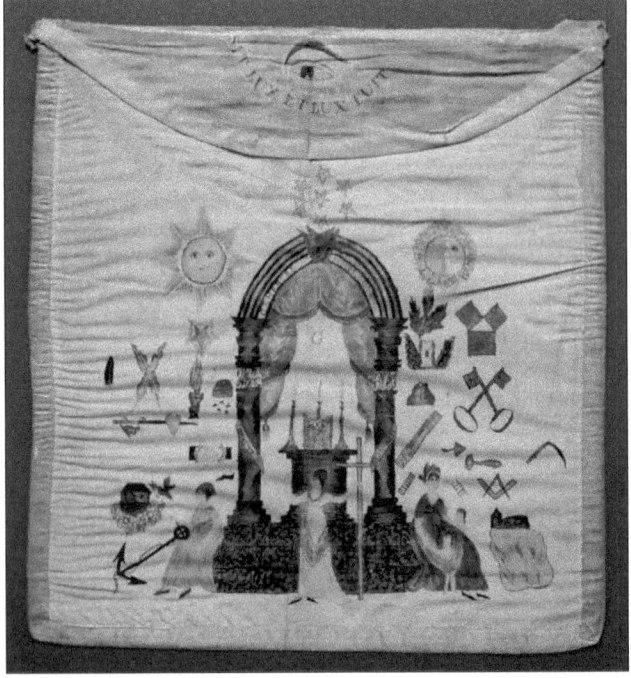

The early-19th-century Masonic apron of Aaron Clark of Hampton No. 111 is painted with Masonic symbols on silk. An apron is the badge of a brother worn at every lodge meeting, and during the early years of American Freemasonry, many were personalized with contemporary folk art for local civic events. Hampton No. 111 met in the attic of brothers Aaron and secretary Moses Clark on the corner of Division and Union Streets. The Clark brothers were born in Stonington, Connecticut, and were veterans of the Revolutionary War. (WL.)

This is the 1804 ledger from Hampton Lodge No. 111. A ledger is a detailed record of the lodge membership, including names, dates, dues notices, reimbursements, initiation dates, and death notices. All the entries were handwritten by lodge secretary Brother Moses Clark. Constituted on July 26, 1804, Hampton No. 111 finally surrendered its charter in 1832 after several years of struggling to remain active. (WL.)

The history is lost on this elaborate Masonic apron in the archives of Paumanok–Port Washington No. 855. Hand-painted on a mix of materials including leather and silk, this blue lodge apron dates to the early 19th century. Many early Masonic aprons are fine works of art, stemming from an intimate collaboration between a Mason and an artist, many of whom were non-Masons or women. (PPWL.)

The Masonic certificate of Brother John H. Jarvis, founding member and the first junior warden of Jephtha No. 494 in Huntington, is seen here. Dated September 27, 1861, the full-color certificate measures 18 by 18 inches and is signed by W∴ William H. King, master; Jesse Carll, senior warden; Ezra W. Seaman, junior warden; and Stephen C. Rogers, secretary. Displaying almost 100 Masonic symbols, this certificate was donated to Jephtha No. 494 by Brother Jarvis's great-grandchildren on April 24, 1963. (JL.)

The past master medallion of W∴ Jonas Pearsall was presented on December 24, 1866, at his conclusion of three consecutive terms as master of Jephtha No. 494. W∴ Pearsall was the third master of Jephtha No. 494 and served a total of four terms leading the lodge (1864–1866, 1871). Part of the first class of five master Masons raised in Jephtha in 1860, Pearsall was a longtime resident of Huntington and a successful local tailor. This medallion is presented to an outgoing master in appreciation of his devotion to the lodge. The sun in the center of the compass and protractor represents light, as the master of a lodge is a source of Masonic light. (JL.)

The Chamber of Reflection is a small, darkened anteroom adjoining the lodge room. The room pictured is at Suffolk No. 60 in Port Jefferson, but most Chambers of Reflection have similar layouts. It is a place where candidates are prepared and meditate just prior to being initiated into Freemasonry or a higher degree. The room may include several items, including candles, an hourglass, bread, and water.

During the period in the Chamber of Reflection, a candidate is given a series of questions, including his duties to God, family, community, and himself. When the candidate is ready, the master of ceremonies knocks three times and leads the initiates into the lodge room for their degree.

This is a view of the senior warden's station in the west of the lodge room in Alcyone No. 695 at 162 Main Street, Northport. Alcyone moved into this third-floor room soon after the building was completed in 1875 but did not add the permanent fixtures until after the lodge purchased the building in 1916. Alcyone No. 695 has been meeting in this room continuously for over 145 years, the longest use of a Masonic lodge on Long Island. (DM.)

The master's station in the east of the lodge room in Alcyone No. 695 in Northport is seen here. The worshipful master sits in the center chair, with the chaplain seated to his left. The brother elected to record the minutes is the secretary and is seated behind the desk on the right. The treasurer, the brother elected to manage the finances, is seated behind the desk on the left. The lodge charter can be seen directly in front of the master's podium, and the two chairs on the lower level are the stations of the senior deacon (left) and marshal. (DM.)

Here is a wide view from the northwest corner of Alcyone No. 695 in Northport, the oldest lodge room on Long Island. The altar in the middle has a Bible placed on top, opened to specific sections of the Old Testament depending on the degree the lodge is opened at. Freemasons are nonsectarian, and a holy book specific to a brother's religion is used during degree ceremonies, including the Torah, Koran, and many other religious texts. (DM.)

This is a close-up view of the junior warden's station in the south of Alcyone No. 695 in Northport. To the left of the gavel is one of two warden columns. When a lodge is at labor during a meeting, the senior warden's column is standing upright, while the junior warden's is down. At refreshment, when the master calls for a brief interval of the meeting, the senior warden's column is placed down, while the junior warden's is upright. The warden column ritual dates to 1760 but is rarely used today in Long Island Freemasonry. (DM.)

Peconic No. 349 sold its Main Street, Greenport building in 2006 and rented Mechanics Hall a few blocks away until 2018, when they moved 23 miles west to the Riverhead Masonic Lodge. Pictured on the next few pages are the only known photographs of the beautiful lodge room interior. At left is the master's station, with the letter "G" several inches from the wall. The early-20th-century hand-painted murals depict the building of King Solomon's temple.

The door from the Chamber of Reflection in Peconic No. 349 in Greenport is seen here, with the twin pillars of Boaz and Jachin, with spinning globes on top. The circular staircase led to a second-floor balcony for brothers to sit when lodge meetings were overflowing. Hand-painted on the walls throughout the lodge room are various images of Masonic symbolism. All the artwork was painted over after the building was sold.

This is a view of the junior warden's station in the old Peconic lodge room in Greenport, with a painted view of the southern outskirts of ancient Jerusalem, the area where King Solomon's temple was constructed by operative masons in 587 BCE.

The senior warden's station in the west of the Peconic No. 349 lodge room in Greenport is pictured here. The mural displays the three Masonic graces—Faith, Hope, and Charity—the three moral principles of Freemasonry. Two are holding important tools of operative and speculative Masons: a square and a level.

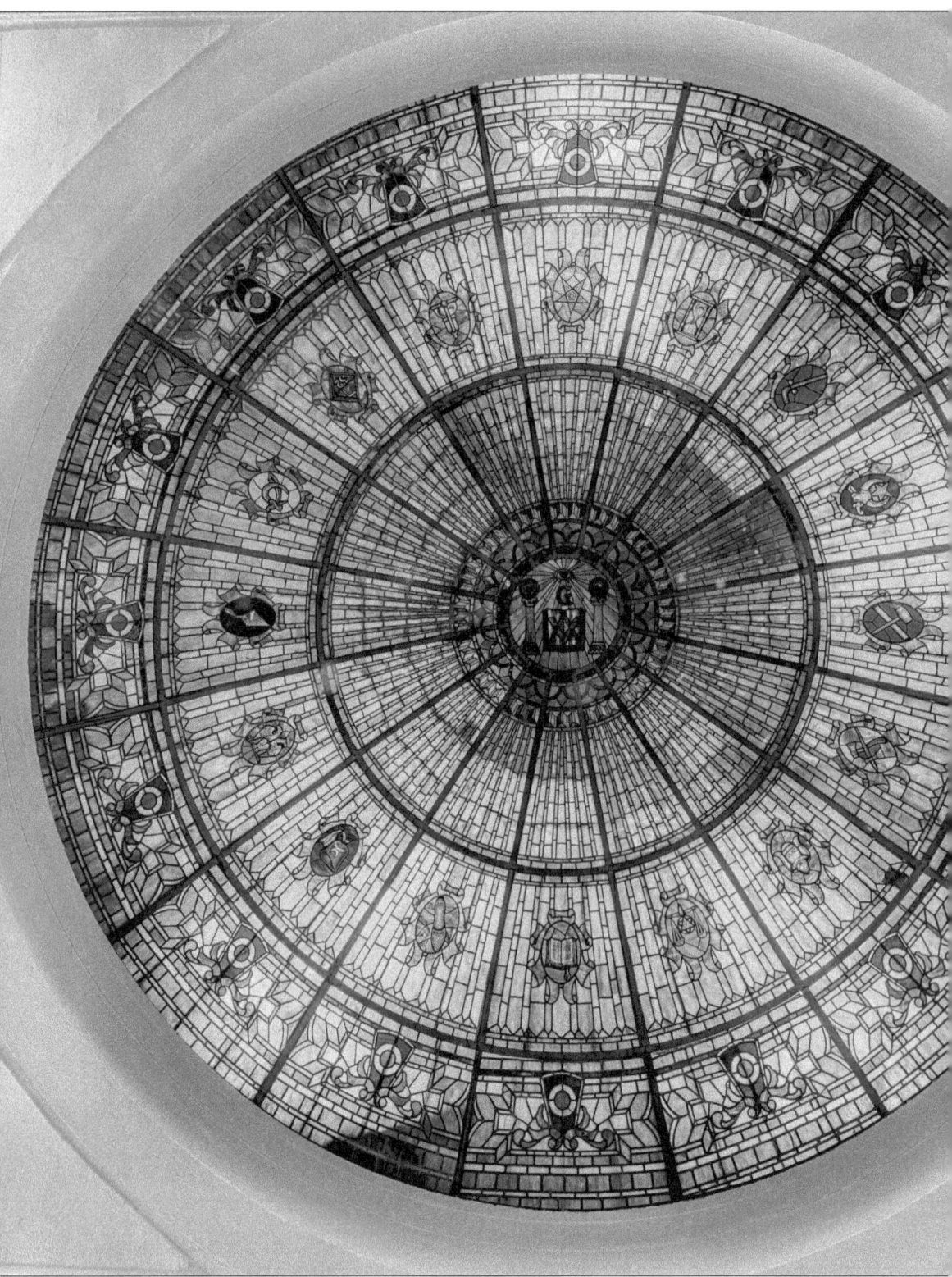

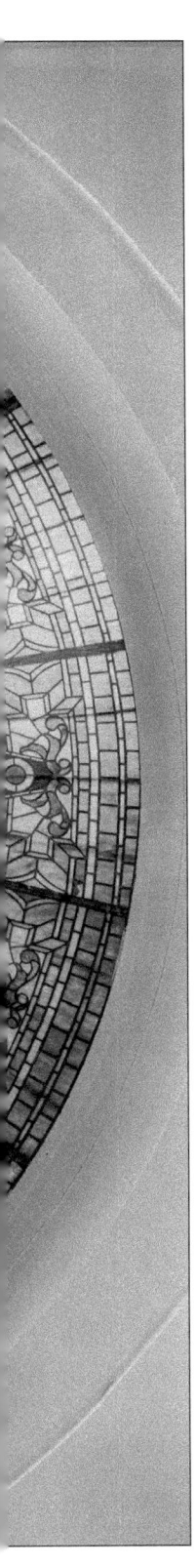

Installed in the late 1920s above the lodge room altar in Long Beach toward the end of the popular stained-glass era is this magnificent dome adorned with intricate Masonic symbols. Measuring approximately 20 feet in circumference, the dome has 16 panels, each with hinges attached for easy cleaning and repair. The dome is installed in an angled steel frame in a separate second-floor room, with ballast lights illuminating the glass. Each of the over 6,000 glazed glass pieces is tinted in a variety of colors, displaying several Masonic symbols. In the center is the all-seeing eye, the letter "G," a holy book, square and compass, and the twin pillars of Boaz and Jachin. Each of the outer sections is adorned with keystones, a symbol of the Royal Arch of the York Rite. By the time of the dome's construction, it was common for stained-glass pieces to be without an artist's signature, and without a dedication plaque, the source of this piece has not been determined. Long Beach No. 1048 sold its building in the late 1970s to a local community center with the unrestored dome completely intact, where it has been a source of enjoyment for children in a daycare center for over 40 years. (DM.)

Seen here is a closeup image of three of the panels in Long Beach depicting several Masonic symbols. On the left is a trowel, a symbolic tool to spread kindness and affection, which binds the members of the Masonic family. The double-headed eagle is the symbol of the Scottish Rite, representing that man is composed of body and spirit and that both good and evil exist in the world. The fez hat on the right is worn by Shriners at various functions, such as parades and outings. (DM.)

These are three additional closeups of the stained-glass dome in Long Beach. On the left is a level, the jewel of the senior warden, which is a symbol of the equality of the brothers in the lodge when at labor. The center design represents two important degrees of the Scottish Rite: the 14th and 32nd. The 14th degree is the final part of the Lodge of Perfection, and the 32nd is the final degree of the rite. On the far right is a variation of the scimitar and crescent of the Mystic Shrine.

These three symbols include the Bible on the left, a scale in the middle, and the Mokanna head from the Grotto on the right. The Mystic Order of the Veiled Prophets of the Enchanted Realm (MOVPER, or the Grotto) is a social organization for master Masons dating to the late 19th century, where members wear a black fez with a red tassel and the Mokanna head embroidered in the middle. In 1917, the Mysterious Order Witches of Salem, a female auxiliary, was founded. In 1949, the Grottoes of North America created a national charitable program focusing on cerebral palsy and dental care for children. (DM.)

On the left is the Knight of the Royal Axe, or as it is known in the Northern Jurisdiction of the Scottish Rite, Prince of Libanus of the 22nd degree. At center is the 24-inch gauge and gavel, part of the three degrees of Master Mason. On the right is the symbol for the Ancient Arabic Order of the Nobles of the Mystic Shrine, also known as the Shriners. (DM.)

Seen here is a Masonic Blue Lodge hand-painted apron with white silk on homespun cloth. Created by an unknown artist, based on the craftwork and materials, this 17-by-14.5-inch apron is estimated to have been made between 1775 and 1800. The apron depicts the altar approached by three steps with the Three Great Lights, the representative of the three lesser lights, two hands, and the five-pointed star between the Ionic columns. On the left is a blazing sun, level, hourglass, and trowel; on the right is a cluster of seven stars around the crescent moon, plumb, ladder, sword pointed toward a naked heart, and anchor. (PPWL.)

Seen here is a royal arch apron with white silk trimmed with red, on a mosaic pavement, seven steps, a stone altar with three great lights, and a radiant all-seeing eye above the clouds on the upper flap. From the collection of W∴ Frederick Tanner of Paumanok No. 855, based on the materials and embroidery, it is estimated that this 14-by-16-inch apron was made between 1825 and 1850. (PPWL.)

This bronze gavel depicting a lion's paw was presented to Massapequa No. 822 in 1917 by W∴ William H. Knoche. Equipped with a fiber striking pad and wooden handle adorned with metallic decorations, the gavel measures 12 inches high with a four-inch circular base. Knoche was employed at the Mitchell Vance Company, where he practiced the trade of chasing metal. Designed by Robert Yelverton Barrows, a New Jersey Mason, from bronze pieces removed from the original gas light fixtures at the old Grand Lodge on Twenty-Third Street, New York City, when they were converted to electricity, the gavel is now part of the Lynbrook-Massapequa No. 822 archives. (LML.)

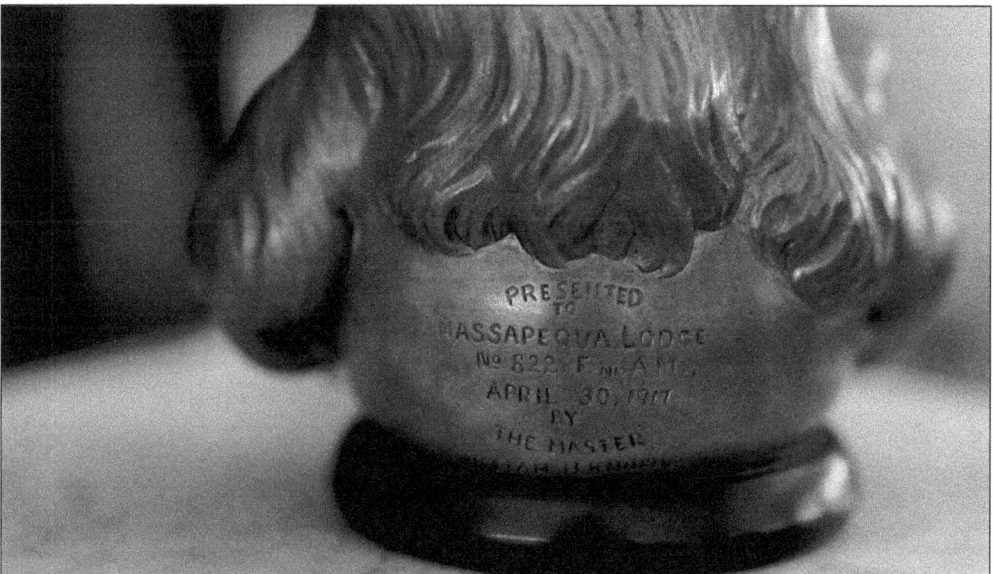

A piece of synthetic fiber from the back of an electrical switchboard was given to a plumber's apprentice to hammer out on an anvil. The apprentice hammered the base until his arm was tired, but he could not crack or dent the fiber piece. From here, W∴ Knoche fashioned the striking base, which has been used for over 100 years. W∴ Knoche also designed the wooden handle and metal fittings. (LML.)

Embroidered silk on velvet, this 1890 Masonic apron from the archives of Wamponamon No. 437 was most likely embroidered by the wife of a brother and worn in a Sag Harbor parade and other public celebrations. The lodge seal shows an Indian paddling his canoe *wamponamon*, or in the English translation, "to the eastward." (WL.)

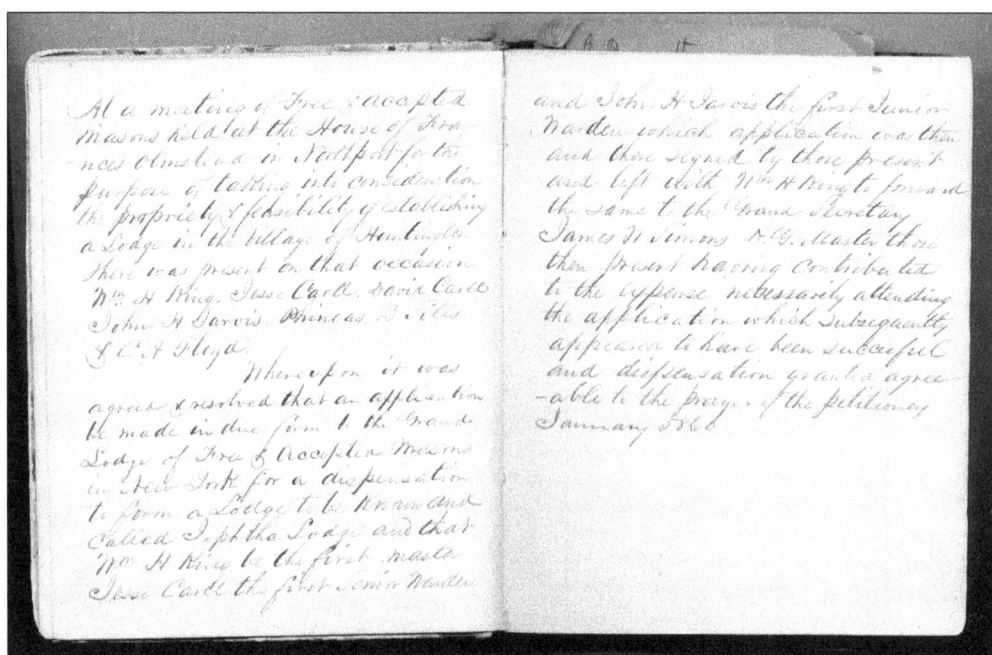

The first two pages of the first minute book for Jephtha No. 494 in Huntington are pictured here. Every lodge meeting has an elected secretary who records the meeting minutes, records, correspondences, and other announcements and preserves them for the lodge archives. Held at the home of Francis Olmstead of Northport in January 1860, the minutes' record "the feasibility of establishing a Lodge in the Village of Huntington," and list the six founders of Jephtha No. 494.

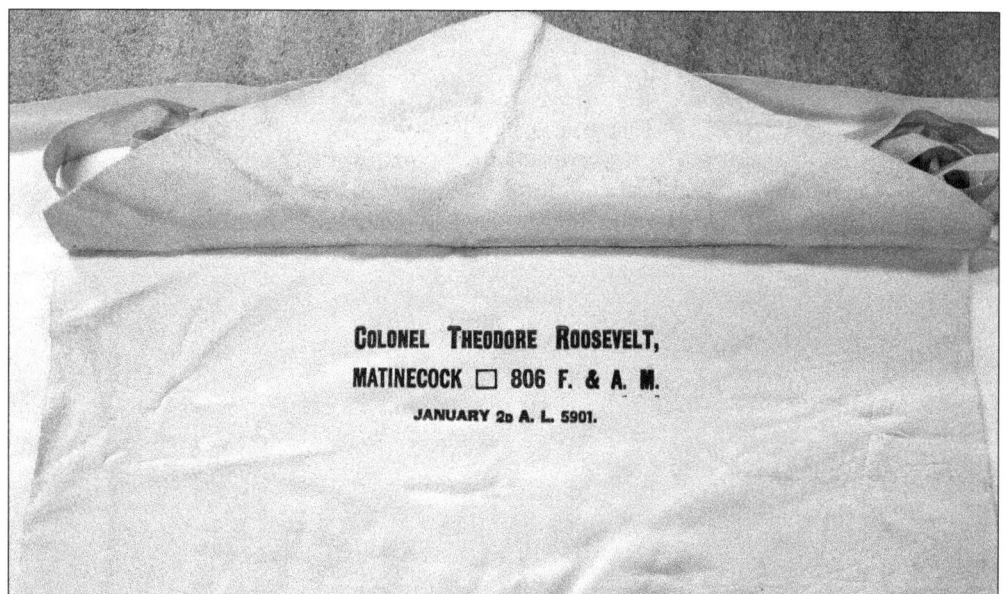

On January 2, 1901, vice president–elect Theodore Roosevelt was initiated to the degree of entered apprentice at Matinecock No. 806 in Oyster Bay, two days after leaving the office of governor of New York. Part of the ceremony includes the presentation of a white lambskin apron to a new Brother, an emblem of innocence and badge of a Mason, to be placed on his coffin after his passing. Brother Roosevelt never had a Masonic funeral service; this apron is in the archives at the Sagamore Hill National Historic Site. (SAG.)

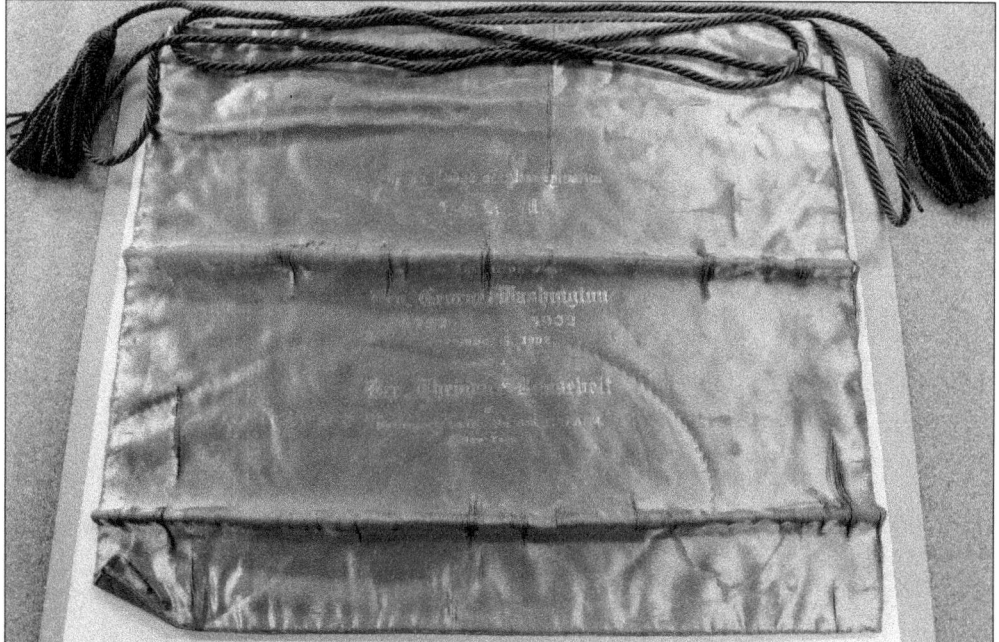

On November 5, 1902, Pres. Theodore Roosevelt delivered a speech to the Grand Lodge of Masons of Pennsylvania, commemorating the sesquicentennial anniversary of the initiation of Brother George Washington in 1752. The Grand Lodge presented this blue Masonic apron to Brother Roosevelt in appreciation for his support of the craft. (SAG.)

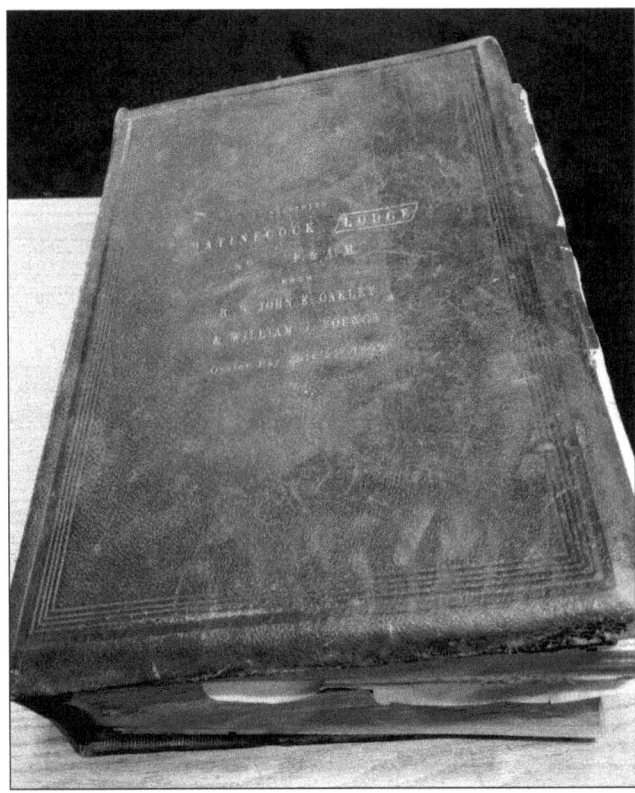

This Bible was presented to Matinecock No. 806 from charter members R∴W∴ John K. Oakley and William Jones Youngs on July 27, 1892. The Bible does not list the lodge number since it was ordered prior to constituting Matinecock No. 806. Oakley was raised in Acanthus No. 719 in Brooklyn, and Young was raised in Anchor No. 729 in College Point and affiliated at Jephtha No. 494 in Huntington. William J. Youngs was the personal secretary of Theodore Roosevelt during his term as governor of New York and Queens district attorney from 1896 to 1899. (DM.)

First used in the rooms above the Van Size market on South Street, Oyster Bay, the Bible was retired on November 19, 1958, after years of usage. Known as the "TR Bible," this is the edition used for all three degrees of Brother Theodore Roosevelt in 1901. Severely damaged in a fire on October 25, 2003, this Bible is rarely used today. (ML.)

The Theodore Roosevelt Memorial Window in Matinecock No. 806 in Oyster Bay was dedicated on December 8, 1926, commemorating the 25th anniversary of Brother Roosevelt's raising to the degree of master Mason. Originally installed behind the master's station in the east, the window was designed and built by local artisan Oliver Smith in his Oyster Bay garage as well as the stained-glass windows in Christ's Church in Oyster Bay. The window depicts a fully armored knight standing on an escalated rock; his flag is furled, and his sword is sheathed, signifying peace with honor, but he stands ready for battle with the enemies of righteousness. The inscription "Theodore Roosevelt, 1901–1919" is inscribed at the bottom between two presidential eagles. The window was severely damaged in a fire in 2003, and the surviving pieces were restored with newly fabricated stained glass and installed with a lightbox in the symbolic north side of the lodge room, where it is displayed today.

Standing over 19 feet high, 10 feet wide, and 6 feet deep in the east of the Oyster Bay lodge room is this elaborate structure closely representing an altarpiece of a Gothic church. The hand-carved furniture in black walnut was custom made for Ancient Landmarks No. 441 F. & A.M. by T. Hersee and Sons in Buffalo, the last surviving set from this 19th-century company. Completed in 1868, the enormous design was delivered before reconstruction of the new lodge room was completed after the fire of 2003, because the wall-mounted piece could not fit through any standard doors. Three chairs reside up against the structure, with the center chair reserved for the worshipful master and the chair just to the right for the chaplain. The other three chairs are for special guests or visiting dignitaries. Embedded within the gable is a colorful circular glass translucent piece with the emblem of the Order of the Eastern Star. Toward the rear and suspended from the small ceiling is the letter "G" found in all Masonic lodges. Both floor-to-ceiling suspension columns have four-light electric candelabra, converted from gas, with paper shades.

The senior warden's station in the west of the lodge room in Matinecock No. 806 is seen here. To the left is the junior deacon's chair, and the two red leather upholstered chairs are reserved for the junior and senior master of ceremonies. The senior warden chair has two lower chairs attached on each side, reserved for visiting dignitaries. The door to the Chamber of Reflection is on the right, from which candidates are led through the pillars of Boaz and Jachin. Above the warden's chair is a balcony where the Matinecock archives and library reside.

The junior warden's station in the south of Matinecock No. 806 is a miniature version of the master's area in the east, complete with a smaller overhang and dark red velvet drapes. The two chairs with staves belong to the stewards of the lodge, brothers who assist the junior warden in providing refreshments to the members.

The altar, three candle stands, and padded kneeling benches in Matinecock No. 806 in Oyster Bay are pictured here. Carved in black walnut like the rest of the furniture in Matinecock No. 806, the intricate Victorian-era centerpiece has six Gothic style arches adorned around the altar with four handcrafted lion heads on each base corner. The profile engraving near the top of the altar is of Thompson Hersee Jr., owner of the furniture design company.

This is a very rare example of three past master chairs in the northeast of the Matinecock lodge room in Oyster Bay. Constructed for Ancient Landmarks No. 441 in 1868, these chairs have the protractor and compass with sun emblems, representing a past master who has observed the rising, meridian height, and setting of the sun while sitting in the east. In most Masonic jurisdictions, past masters do not have an officially assigned seat in the lodge room.

This is a close-up view of the finely carved engraving on each of the nine benches in Matinecock No. 806. Using a Gothic style design combining the letters "A" and "L," representing Ancient Landmarks No. 441 in Buffalo, the lodge that commissioned the design and construction in the 1860s of all of the furniture in the Oyster Bay lodge room.

This is a view of the lodge room from the second-floor balcony/library at Matinecock No. 806 in Oyster Bay.

89

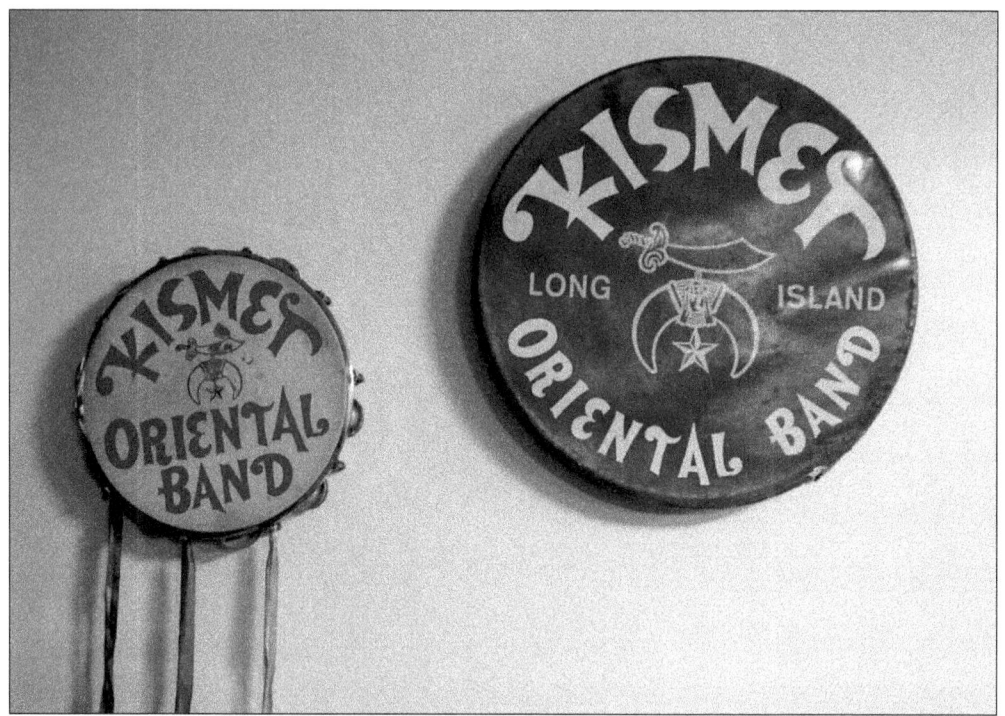

Shrine Oriental bands date to the 1893 Chicago World's Fair, when nobles of the Chicago Medinah Shrine were impressed that two Turks could entertain a large gathering with just a musette and a tom-tom. After the first band was formed in 1896, the popularity expanded to other shrines, which marched in parades and assisted as ceremonial guards for degrees and in performances for other organizations. (KS.)

All Masonic organizations send out regular printed communication to their members to keep them informed on the latest events. The most elaborate newsletters are printed by the Kismet Shrine, managed by the illustrious potentate. This front cover from December 29, 1921, depicts jolly old St. Nick, who happens to be a Shriner, throwing various candidates (note the armbands) from different backgrounds out of a blimp and into the Kismet Shrine. (KS.)

The Parade of the Wooden Soldiers (also known as the Parade of the Tin Soldiers) has been performed at the *Christmas Spectacular Starring the Radio City Rockettes* in Rockefeller Center in New York City since 1933. It is based on an instrumental musical character piece written by German composer Leon Jessel in 1897. The Wooden Soldiers of Kismet Temple have marched in many parades in their stiff red coats with crossed white bands and their faces powdered white with large pink circles on their cheeks. The Kismet Wooden Soldier unit is the only one sanctioned by the Radio City Rockettes to perform or parade in these classic outfits. (Both, KS.)

This series of three acrylic portraits by Yelana Elefante is on display above the junior warden's station at Spartan Lodge in Baldwin. Inspired by the Italian artist Tintoretto, the classical-style pieces took a total of nine weeks to complete by Elefante, who completed her training at Moscow State University. Although Freemasonry is not a religion, the three seven-by-four-foot panels contain symbolism from the three Masonic degrees inspired by religious allegories. (SL.)

The first of three panels by Yelana Elefante shows Saint John the Baptist, inspired by the 1540 painting by the Italian Renaissance artist Titian (also known as Tiziano Vecelli). In this piece, Saint John is on the River Jordan on the first step of entered apprentice. The symbol on top is a plumb, an instrument used by stonemasons to determine how well aligned a vertical surface is; in Freemasonry, it is used as a symbol of upright behavior among brothers and is the jewel worn by the junior warden. (SL.)

The middle panel depicts the three, five, and seven steps of the Fellowcraft degree and the symbol for a level. The winding steps are in the Middle Chamber of King Solomon's temple, part of a lecture in the Fellowcraft degree. The level is the jewel of the senior warden and represents equality of the members when meeting in the lodge. (SL.)

The third panel shows John the Evangelist next to an acacia plant with King Solomon's temple in the background. The patron saints of Freemasons are John the Baptist and John the Evangelist; Masons hold annual festivals honoring both saints. Masons have made the observance of these annual festivals universal by removing the Christian dogma. The first Grand Lodge of England was organized on the Festival Day of the Baptist in 1717. (SL.)

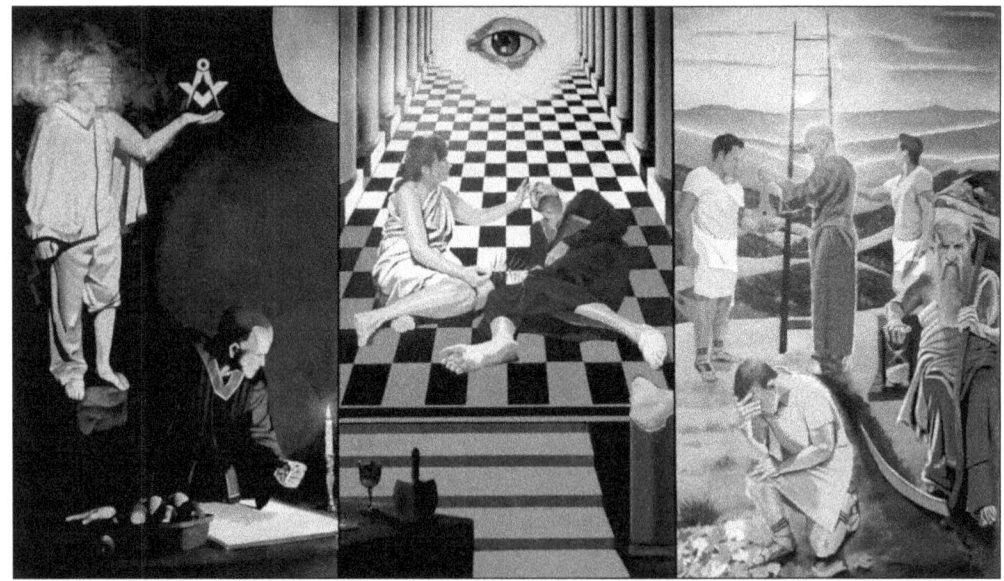

Seen here are three oil-on-canvas portraits by Brother Matthew Tyree, son of R∴W∴ Charles P. Tyree, past master of Spartan No. 956, grand sword bearer of New York Masons from 2000 to 2002 and district grand lecturer of the Order of the Eastern Star. The panels, on display in the symbolic north wall of the Spartan No. 956 lodge room in Baldwin, show the artist's self-reflection on his progression through the three degrees of Masonry. Brother Tyree was a past state master counselor of the DeMolay and 20-year member of Spartan No. 956.

The first piece by Brother Tyree is of a candidate holding a 24-inch gauge waiting in the Chamber of Reflection prior to the first degree. The moon and candlelight represent light the candidate is about to receive in Masonry. The man at the table is Grand Master Hiram Abiff with the unfinished trestle board of the temple, looking over his shoulder for any cowans and eavesdroppers. The basket of apples represent pomegranates on the pillars of Jachin and Boaz.

The second piece represents Hiram Abiff after he was murdered for not revealing the secrets of the craft, with the weeping virgin holding a sprig of acacia, distraught over the dead architect and the incomplete temple. All three pieces display different shades of red, symbolizing the three degrees. The first uses crimson as a warning of approaching danger, the second has more of a blood-red for the grand master's death, and the third has a more vibrant red, symbolizing love.

The third panel shows two Masons, one holding a trowel and the other a level, standing with Hiram Abiff just prior to his ascension on Jacob's Ladder, with the outskirts of Jerusalem in the background. The ladder's nine rungs symbolize each virtue for resurrection prior to ascension to heaven. The man in the foreground is kneeling at the last known location of the remains of Hiram Abiff, kneeling in the style DeMolay use in prayer for their rituals. Father Time is holding an hourglass, representing the limited time in a person's life. The artist used his father, R∴W∴ Charles P. Tyree, as the model for Father Time.

"Wamponamon" was created by Brother John Philip Capello with assistant painter Linda Capello and Brother Francois Bourdrez, rigger. This mural was completed within two months in the summer of 2014 over the worshipful master's station in the east in Wamponamon Lodge in Sag Harbor. Capello is a self-taught sculptor and painter and a member of many professional affiliations, including the National Society of Mural Painters, Artist Alliance of East Hampton, and Southampton Artists Association. His oil paintings and stone sculptures are extensively represented in over 100 private collections.

Capello's use of surrealism combines several Masonic symbols with the Wamponamon, a Montaukett Native American in a canoe, and the name of the lodge. The mural is in the east of the lodge, a symbolic place in a lodge and for Wamponamon, the Native American definition "into the east." The celestial sky moves from night to day, representing one day, with several stars and specific planets. Masonic icons include an eye-topped pyramid, Bible, key, checkered board, square, and compass.

Four

OYSTER BAY

HOME OF A PRESIDENT AND A BROTHER

In 1888, local master Masons started discussions to petition for a dispensation to form a lodge in Oyster Bay. Tired of traveling great distances to their current home lodges in Huntington, Glen Cove, and Manhattan, the brothers formed a committee and met at the home of their secretary, Dr. George W. Faller, on the corner of White and East Main Streets.

For several years, it was required that local lodges draft a resolution to form a new lodge within a territorial jurisdiction. Despite the unanimous approval of Jephtha in Huntington, Glen Cove made the process difficult for the Oyster Bay residents. The Grand Lodge of New York rejected the application four times because of Glen Cove's demands, and it was not until July 6, 1892, that all disputes were settled and Matinecock No. 806 F. & A.M. was granted a dispensation to form a lodge.

Matinecock was translated from Native American as "at the hilly land," perfectly describing Long Island's north shore. The Matinecock Native American communities lived along the north shore bays and inlets, containing 20 to 30 family groups. They assisted the first Dutch settlers with farming and harvesting shellfish. It was assumed, but never confirmed, that the lodge was named by its first master, Commodore William Lincoln Swan. Brother Swan had an avid interest in the local history and was even one of the founders of the Seawanhaka Corinthian Yacht Club and named his local florist business Seawanhaka Greenhouses.

Matinecock Lodge is best known as the Masonic home of Brother Theodore Roosevelt. Referred to in the lodge minutes book as "brother" or "guest," Roosevelt enjoyed meetings at Matinecock when he was able to attend in relative secrecy without the fanfare that usually follows a president. Between 1901, when Brother Roosevelt was raised a master Mason, and 1909, when he left the White House, brothers from 147 different lodges from around the world visited Matinecock Lodge, hoping to get a chance to meet the president.

A second lodge also meets in Oyster Bay. Bethpage-Hicksville No. 975 is a combination of several former lodges, including Bethpage No. 975, Hollis No. 922, Manetto No. 1025, Meadow Brook No. 1005, and Mineola No. 985.

The Fleet Building was the second location for Matinecock No. 806. Located on the south side of East Main Street, Oyster Bay, the area was known as "Fleet's Block." Owner Samuel Van Wyck Fleet rented a 30-by-34-foot room above a livery stable to the lodge at an annual rate of $144 for three years. The first meeting at this location was held on December 14, 1892. (JEH.)

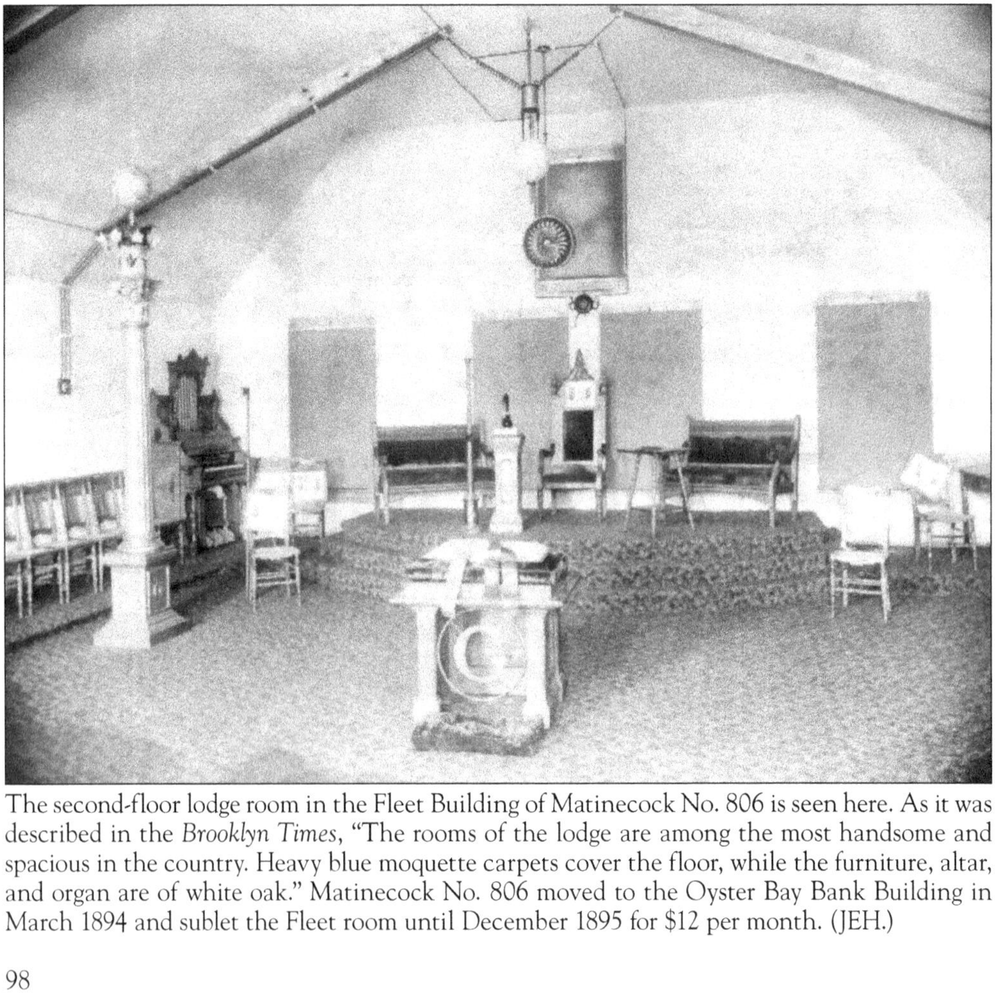

The second-floor lodge room in the Fleet Building of Matinecock No. 806 is seen here. As it was described in the *Brooklyn Times*, "The rooms of the lodge are among the most handsome and spacious in the country. Heavy blue moquette carpets cover the floor, while the furniture, altar, and organ are of white oak." Matinecock No. 806 moved to the Oyster Bay Bank Building in March 1894 and sublet the Fleet room until December 1895 for $12 per month. (JEH.)

Constructed in 1893 on Audrey Avenue by the Oyster Bay Bank, Matinecock No. 806 leased the third floor from 1894 to 1924. The second floor was occupied by the staff of Theodore Roosevelt until 1903. The bank occupied the first floor, and the basement included a pool hall and tobacco shop. In 1927, part of the basement was removed and the building was lowered, eliminating the front stairs. (JEL.)

Seen here is a very early example of electric candles being used around the altar in the lodge room in the Oyster Bay Bank Building in 1901, the year Vice President Roosevelt progressed through his three degrees, becoming a master Mason. On the evening of Brother Roosevelt's raising on April 24, 1901, it was estimated that over 500 visitors were present, but only master Masons with tickets were allowed entry to witness the historic event. (JEL.)

Theodore Roosevelt is seen here dressed as a master of a Masonic lodge, complete with master's apron, jewel, and gavel. Brother Roosevelt never held office in any lodge, and he was unsure if it was due form to wear a worshipful master's regalia. Most likely prompted by local brothers looking to promote the visiting celebrity, this image was staged during Roosevelt's campaign for president while with the Bull Moose Party in 1912. Photographed in Spokane, Washington, at Oriental Lodge No. 74 and wearing regalia from Spokane Lodge No. 34, this is the only known photograph of the former president as a Mason. A reader with a photographic memory and completing all three degrees within 16 weeks, Brother Roosevelt was so proficient in the ritual for the entered apprentice degree that he corrected the brothers conducting the examination when they stumbled before being passed to the degree of fellowcraft. Brother Roosevelt's third-degree sideliners included M∴W∴ Charles W. Mead, grand master, and seven past grand masters from New York and Connecticut. Although he was unable to attend regular communications at Matinecock No. 806 due to the lack of meetings during the summer months when he stayed at Sagamore Hill during his presidency, Brother Roosevelt thoroughly enjoyed the brotherhood and visited several lodges around the country and presided over the Masonic cornerstone laying for the House of Representatives office building in Washington, DC. (LOC.)

The officers of Matinecock No. 806 are pictured in 1904. From left to right are (first row) Alfred Ludlam; W∴ James Duthie; Rev. Henry Homer Washburn, and Rev. Alexander Gatherer Russell; (second row) Frank Spicer, George Downing, Edward Waldron, Thomas E. Baldwin, John Bingham, Stephen Bayles, James Buchanan, and Charles Hill. (JEH.)

James Duthie was master of Matinecock Lodge from 1902 to 1904 and the senior warden when Theodore Roosevelt progressed through his three degrees, although visiting dignitaries sat in most of the officers' chairs for the vice president's degrees. Duthie was the gardener of the Townsend Estate and was an acquaintance of Roosevelt. W∴ Duthie is pictured as a member of the Nassau Commandery No. 73 of the Knights Templar. (JEH.)

Matinecock No. 806 purchased four lots on Maxwell Avenue in 1911 with the intention of erecting a building. The property was sold in 1921 after World War I delayed planning and construction. The former Townsend Inn (also known as Oyster Bay Inn) was purchased in 1923 by Matinecock No. 806 for $30,000. Constructed in 1902, the project was supervised by Charles DeKay Townsend on the former site of Jacob Townsend's home dating to the mid-18th century.

The former Oyster Bay Inn had 53 guest rooms on three floors, a fully functional restaurant, café, and rathskeller. Extensive renovations took place, including removal of the seven gables, remodeling of the guest rooms, removal of the third floor, and construction of a new lodge room on the second floor. (JEH.)

The first communication for Matinecock No. 806 in its new location at 14 West Main Street, Oyster Bay, was held on September 3, 1924. During the Depression, Matinecock Lodge loaned out some rooms in the rear annex to destitute brothers. This image shows the lodge with the rear annex as it appeared in 1933. The annex was demolished in the 1970s and is now a parking lot. (JEH.)

This is a view of the master's station in the east of the Matinecock lodge room. Situated above the three chairs is the Theodore Roosevelt Memorial Window, a large stained-glass window designed by local artist Oliver Smith and installed in 1926. Commemorating the 25th anniversary of the raising of Brother Roosevelt, the piece depicts a knight in full armor, with his sword sheathed and flag furled, depicting a desire for peace with honor. (JEH.)

Here is a wide view of the Matinecock lodge room in 1940, with the Theodore Roosevelt Memorial Window behind the master's station in the east. The junior warden's chair can be seen on the right, with the altar in the center. Officer's aprons are placed on their respective chairs throughout the room. (ML.)

The symbolic west in the Matinecock lodge room is seen as it appeared in 1940. A pipe organ is in the loft just above the senior warden's station. This organ was donated to Manetto Lodge No. 1025 in Hicksville in 1950 and replaced with a new Hammond organ, dedicated as the R∴W∴ James Duthie Memorial Organ. (JEH.)

Seen here is Youngs Memorial Cemetery on Cove Road in Oyster Bay, the final resting place for Brother Theodore Roosevelt. Traditionally, all Masons in good standing are allowed a Masonic funeral service, but none took place at Roosevelt's gravesite in 1919. Brother Roosevelt's Masonic apron is stored in the archives at the Sagamore Hill National Historic Site. (JEH.)

A military detachment stood guard over Brother Roosevelt's grave several weeks after his internment on January 8, 1919. On January 29, a special communication of Matinecock No. 806 was held as a memorial service. A resolution was adopted in commemoration of our "illustrious brother," requiring that "the Lodge Room be draped in mourning for the period of 60 days." Several lodges sent delegations, including Jephtha No. 494, Morton No. 63, and Suffolk No. 60. (JEH.)

Since 1947, the New York State League of Masonic Clubs and the National League of Masonic Clubs honors the memory of Brother Theodore Roosevelt. The public service begins at Matinecock Lodge, and a pilgrimage continues to Roosevelt's grave at Youngs Cemetery. In 1959, the services changed from the anniversary of Roosevelt's death in January to April, commemorating his raising as a master Mason on April 24, 1901. Pictured is the ceremony from April 27, 2019.

The first of two state historical markers for a Long Island Masonic lodge is in front of what is affectionately known as the "President's Lodge" in Oyster Bay. Although Brother Roosevelt never attended lodge meetings in the current lodge purchased by Matinecock No. 806 over four years after his death, the building displays significant artifacts relating to the president's Masonic career.

On October 25, 2003, a devastating fire burned down a considerable portion of Matinecock Lodge in Oyster Bay. Despite the horrendous damage, several fire departments and lodge members saved the lodge charter, by-laws, original membership record books, and the Bible Brother Theodore Roosevelt took his obligation of Master Mason on. Due to the extensive damage, the building was demolished and rebuilt using the original layout after a ground-breaking ceremony on October 15, 2005.

Chartered in 1858, Ancient Landmarks No. 441 met at 318 Pearl Street in Buffalo starting in 1905. After the 2003 fire at Matinecock No. 806, several Masonic lodges donated funds, furniture, artifacts, and literature to assist in the rebuilding efforts. In 2005, Ancient Landmarks No. 441 was unable to house the complete set and voted to transfer the furniture to Matinecock No. 806 with revisionary rights to Ancient Landmarks, provided Matinecock uses the furniture in an active Masonic lodge. All the pieces were sent to Oyster Bay except the lamb statue atop the master's station. (ML.)

In 1920, a group of 34 master Masons met in Arcanum Hall on Main and Conklin Streets to petition Grand Lodge to create a lodge in Farmingdale. Chartered on June 11, 1921, Bethpage No. 975 purchased a 1902 building at 125 Main Street, Farmingdale, from the Odd Fellows for $6,000, and with Bethpage O.E.S. No. 651, the Masons purchased the adjoining lot for $1,200. Suburbia No. 1152 of Levittown met here from 1956 to 1972. The Masons sold the building in 1970 to the Knights of Pythias. (FBHS.)

In December 1965, Bethpage No. 975 started the process of purchasing land to erect a larger building. In 1972, two parcels on Conklin Street were purchased, leaving a clear field for the erection of the new temple at 197 Fulton Street in Farmingdale. Bethpage No. 975 met on Fulton Street from 1972 to 1995 before moving to the Hicksville Masonic Temple on 19 Nicholai Street. In 2009, Bethpage No. 975 merged with Mineola No. 985 to what is now Bethpage-Hicksville No. 975. (FBHS.)

From 1942 to 1945, Bethpage No. 975 in Farmingdale was one of only two Masonic service centers on Long Island for military servicemen. Co-sponsored with the Bethpage O.E.S. No. 651, thousands of servicemen were entertained with coffee, cake, books, and games by the Farmingdale Service Organization (FSO). All the items were donated to the service center, and the Bethpage brothers received letters of gratitude from the deployed servicemen for many years. The second service center on Long Island was only 11 miles away, where Jephtha No. 494 in Huntington entertained 6,447 servicemen. (Both, FBHS.)

A new lodge in eastern Nassau County was spearheaded by the father of Manetto Lodge No. 1025's first master, W:. Adolph G. Rave, and his father, a past master at Hearter Lodge in Brooklyn, who desired to form a lodge in Hicksville. The elder Rave passed away before seeing his wish fulfilled, but the land the present building stands on was donated by the late brother's widow in accordance with the wishes of her husband. (KS.)

Remodeled in 1964, the lodge room of the Hicksville Masonic Temple at 18 West Nicholai Street is pictured here. Constituted on May 8, 1924, Manetto No. 1025 merged with Meadow Brook No. 1005 in 1995 and was renamed Manetto-Brook No. 1005. In 1997, Hollis No. 922 from the Second Queens District merged with Manetto-Brook No. 1005 and was renamed Manetto-Brook-Hollis No. 922. In 2009, Bethpage No. 975, Mineola No. 985, and Three Pillars No. 1139 merged with Manetto-Brook-Hollis No. 922 and is known today as Bethpage-Hicksville No. 975. (RLML.)

Five

TOWN OF HEMPSTEAD

THE BIRTH OF FREEMASONRY IN NASSAU COUNTY

The Town of Hempstead consists of 22 villages, 37 hamlets, and over 20 Masonic lodges over the past 200 years. Freemasonry in what is now Hempstead began in 1797 with the formation of Morton No. 63. Three of the eight charter members of Morton No. 63 had a strong personal bond with Maj. Gen. Jacob Morton, deputy grand master of Masons in New York, marshal to Brother George Washington's first inauguration, and later, grand master of Masons in New York from 1801 to 1804. Jacob Seaman Jackson and Thomas Carman served as officers during the American Revolution with Morton, and all three were members of the state militia, comprising New York City and Long Island. Whitehead Cornwell was an attorney who served in the New York State Assembly with Morton. These three founding members were instrumental in naming Morton Lodge after their esteemed colleague and brother. The lodge first met in the public tavern in Bedell House from 1797 to 1837, on the northeast corner of Front and Main Streets in Hempstead, adjacent to St. George's Episcopal Church.

Morton No. 63 faced many challenges throughout the 19th century. During a very brief relocation to the home of Brother Riely Raynor in 1837, a fire destroyed several items, but the Morton Bible, jewels, book of minutes, and the lodge warrant were saved. Due to lack of activity, Morton No. 63 surrendered its charter to Grand Lodge in 1842. Morton No. 63 faced further challenges including the Treasurer's Ledger going missing for over 100 years, anti-Masonic sentiment gaining popularity, and two separate splits of the Grand Lodge of New York before the reissue of the Warrant of Morton No. 63 in 1860 after it was issued a warrant as Morton No. 469 from June 1859 to June 1860.

Freemasonry started expanding in Hempstead in 1897 and spread to areas including Baldwin, Bellmore, Floral Park, Freeport, Garden City, Inwood, Lynbrook, Steward Manor, Rockville Centre, Valley Stream, Wantagh, and Woodmere until the 1950s.

Located in the Floyd-Jones Cemetery on the grounds of Old Grace Church on Merrick Road in Massapequa are the graves of R∴W∴ David Richard Floyd-Jones and his wife, Sarah Onderdonk. David was master of Huntington No. 26 in 1796 and a charter member of Morton No. 63. Scion of early settlers Richard Floyd and Thomas Jones, Floyd-Jones inherited the Fort Neck estate in Massapequa previously owned by his exiled Tory uncle Thomas Jones. Born David Richard-Floyd in 1764, his name was appended Floyd-Jones in 1788 as a requirement to inherit property from his exiled ancestor.

At the base of Floyd-Jones's grave is a plaque dedicated to David Richard Floyd-Jones by the Grand Lodge of New York in 1981, commemorating the bicentennial of Freemasonry in New York. Appointed the first worshipful master of Morton No. 63 in 1797, David Richard Floyd-Jones sat in the master's chair for 20 of the next 24 years, until 1820. Floyd-Jones was the third direct descendent of two original English settlers of Long Island and a cousin of William Floyd, one of the signers of the Declaration of Independence.

Morton No. 63 was instituted in the Village of Hempstead, Queens County, on June 23, 1797, and named after R∴W∴ Jacob Morton, deputy grand master of Masons in New York. It was through Morton's friendship with Morton No. 63 founding members Jacob Seaman Jackson, Thomas Carman, and Whitehead Cornwell that the petition was fast-tracked in less than two days. Morton was the marshal for George Washington's first inauguration, and when it was discovered that a Bible was not readily available, he retrieved one from St. John's No. 1, where he was worshipful master at the time. (RLML.)

On June 23, 1897, eleven past masters from Morton No. 63 gathered for a group photograph celebrating the lodge centennial. From left to right are (first row, seated) John W. De Mott, Augustus. R. Griffin, Robert A. Davison, Benjamin A. Haff, and B. Valentine Clowes; (second row, standing) Robert Seabury, Joseph E. Firth, Charles L. Phipps, Augustus Denton, Lott Van De Water Jr., and Oliver E. Stanton. (RLML.)

Morton No. 63 rented the third floor of the new Cohen Building at 40 Main Street in Hempstead from 1893 to 1911. The lodge room was in the front section of the third floor, with a sizable dining room and kitchen in the rear. Modern amenities included gas jets for lights, running water, one toilet, and steam heat from a cellar plant, the first of its kind in Hempstead. (HPL.)

The Cohen Building was owned by Brother Louis Cohen, who maintained a dry goods store on the ground level and lived in an apartment on the second floor. The Cohen Building was widened in 1902, with the addition of new windows on the third floor and a redesign of the second-floor windows. A Masonic square and compass can be seen between the second and third floors. Morton No. 63 remained at this location until 1911. (HPL.)

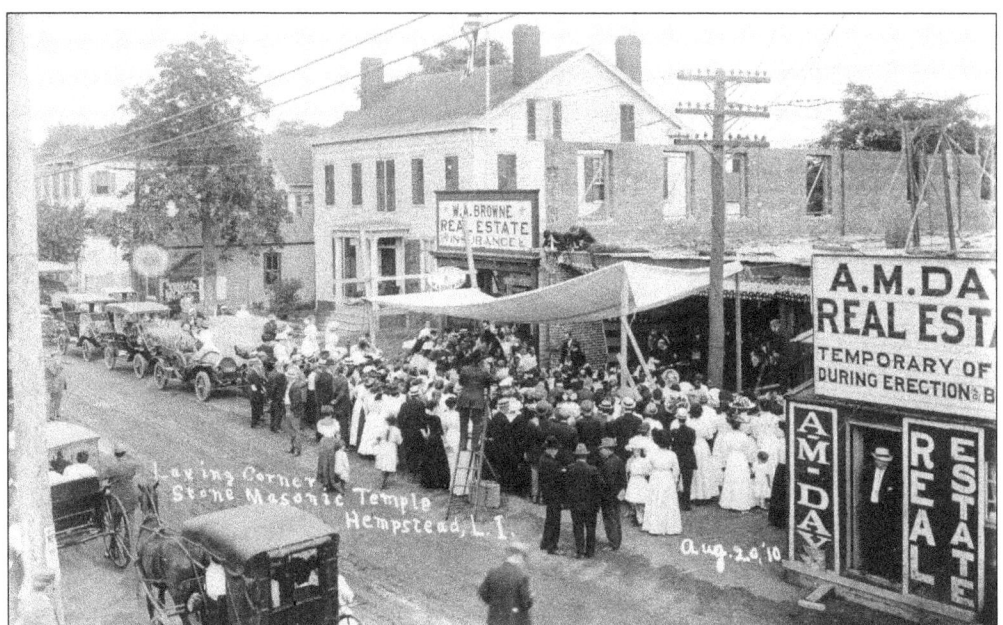

On August 10, 1910, a cornerstone ceremony for a new Masonic lodge was held on the south side of Fulton Avenue east of Main Street in Hempstead. M∴W∴ Robert J. Kenworthy, grand master of Masons in New York, presided over the ceremony, which included a choir of 60 Sunday school children of the Hempstead Methodist Church. (HPL.)

In accordance with Masonic tradition, the cornerstone was proved by the symbolic application of the square, level, and plumb and was consecrated with corn, wine, and oil, symbolizing nourishment, refreshment, and joy. The time capsule placed inside the cornerstone included contemporary records of Morton No. 63, copies of local newspapers including the *Hempstead Sentinel*, *Hempstead Inquirer*, and *New York Herald*, a copy of the Lord's Prayer and a Lincoln-head penny dated 1910. (WML.)

Morton Lodge No. 63 held its first meeting at 298 Fulton Street, Hempstead, on January 9, 1911. Called the Morton Masonic Temple, the building was sold in 1979 and is still in use today as a church. Other lodges met here, including Garden City No. 1083 (1927–1979) and Jamaica No. 546 (1974–1979).

This architectural rendering from 1929 shows a proposed Masonic Temple that Morton No. 63 was planning on the east side of Cathedral Avenue north of Fulton Avenue in Hempstead. Budgeted at $250,000 in 1929, the Gothic structure was designed by William F. McCulloch of Hempstead. By July 1930, a few months after the stock market crash of 1929, the brotherhood voted against raising their annual membership dues from $10 to $20 and elected not to proceed with the project, still owing the architect $6,000 of the original $15,000 fee. (WML.)

Pictured is the dedication of Wantagh No. 1112 Temple on April 22, 1961. In December 1929, at the home of R∴W∴ William H. Becker, the foundation of Wantagh Masonic Association started to take shape. Meeting regularly at the Wantagh firehouse, the brothers later moved to the Parish Hall of the Wantagh Congregational Church on May 14, 1930. The charter for Wantagh No. 1112 was constituted on June 10, 1931. It continued to meet in the parish hall until 1950, when it moved to a building owned by the Bellmore Square Club on Square Place in Bellmore.

In 1954, Wantagh No. 1112 sold an additional piece of real estate on Seaford Avenue to cover the costs of expanding the building on Square Place. With membership reaching nearly 600, the lodge secured a $40,000 mortgage and solicited pledges of bonds from the membership. This financing enabled the construction of a more modern two-story temple around the old Square Club building. The public dedication of Wantagh No. 1112's new Masonic temple was held on April 22, 1961, in Bellmore, with M∴W∴ Carl W. Peterson, grand master of Masons in the state of New York, presiding over the ceremonies. (WML.)

Massapequa No. 822 received its charter in 1897, with the lodge name chosen over Star of the South by one vote. The lodge originally met in a hotel on Village Avenue, just south of the Long Island Rail Road tracks. In 1909, Massapequa No. 822 moved to the third floor of the new Bank of Rockville Centre at the northeast corner of Merrick Road and Village Avenue and remained there until 1920. (RVCPL.)

Past and future masters of Massapequa No. 822 gathered for this group picture in the lodge room in the Bank of Rockville Centre in 1915. Only brothers with numbers are identified. Years in parentheses following each name represent their term in office. From left to right are (first row) No. 13, R∴W∴ John Watts (1908); No. 15, W∴ Samuel W. Conner (1911); No. 18, W∴ Augustus D. Kesley (1903); No. 19, R∴W∴ William H. Connell (1898); and No. 20, W∴ William S. Goyert (1908); (second row) No. 21, W∴ Charles H. Richardson (1919); No. 3, W∴ George J. Birch (1918); No. 12, W∴ William H. Knoche (1917); No. 6, W∴ Smith F. Pearsall (1915); and No. 7, W∴ Walter B. Wellbrock (1916). (LML.)

Despite owning a plot of land on the east side of South Park Avenue south of Merrick Road, Massapequa No. 822 chose to move into the home of the Rockville Centre Club on 28 Lincoln Avenue in Rockville Centre. The original structure was built around 1905 as a community meeting place as well as a place to host basketball games. By 1920, the club was in dire financial straits, leading to the sale of the building to Massapequa No. 822. (LML.)

Several lodges have met in Rockville Centre over the years, including Guiding Light No. 1154, Guiding Light-Olympia No. 808, Oceanside No. 1140, and Jamaica Queens Village No. 546. In 1979, the building was sold to the Long Island Valley of Ancient Accepted Scottish Rite. As of 2020, four lodges meet here: Stewart Manor–St. Albans No. 56, Lynbrook-Massapequa No. 822, South Shore–Long Beach No. 1126, and Valley Stream No. 1143.

The first lodge officers of Lynbrook Lodge No. 1018 are pictured in 1923 where they met above the Lynbrook Movie Theater on Merrick Road. After acquiring a parcel on Earl Avenue and Peninsula Boulevard in 1926, the planned multi-story building was redesigned after the stock market crash of 1929 with reduced square footage. The lodge later sold the building and moved into the Scottish Rite Temple in Rockville Centre. In 1986, Lynbrook No. 1018 merged with Massapequa No. 822 and was renamed Lynbrook-Massapequa No. 822. (LML.)

The Lynbrook Fellowcraft Club dressed for a degree drama on the building of King Solomon's temple, also known as "the First Temple" in ancient Jerusalem. Part of the ritual in the Masonic degrees, a candidate progresses through his journey to obtaining the degree of master Mason. This ritual has been performed for thousands of Masons since the early 18th century. (LML.)

The Freeport Club was located on the west side of South Grove Street, south of Sunrise Highway, and was the first home of Spartan No. 956. Instituted at Odd Fellows Hall on Merrick Road, Freeport, with 87 charter members, including 66 from Massapequa No. 822, Spartan later moved into its own building in 1922, where the lodge remained for the next 55 years. Spartan's godmother lodge was Spartan No. 70 in Spartanburg, South Carolina, where over 200 Spartan brothers of New York were stationed at nearby Camp Wadsworth.

After a devastating fire at the Spartan Masonic Temple on South Grove Street on July 5, 1977, the only remaining artifact is the cornerstone, now outside the Freeport Historical Society at 350 South Main Street. Soon after being displaced, Spartan No. 956 met at Sunrise Masonic Temple on West Merrick Road, Freeport, and the Wantagh Masonic Lodge, Bellmore. Spartan No. 956 later moved to the Baldwin Lodge, later purchasing the building where it continues to meet today. Several lodges later merged with Spartan No. 956 over the years, including Prospect No. 1047 (in 1992), Sunrise-Laurelton No. 1069 (2003), and South Bay No. 1145 (2014).

In June 1914, a dozen Masons residing in Floral Park met at the home of Dr. Thomas F. Davies to discuss organizing a Masonic lodge. After a follow-up meeting at Syme's Hall, the Masonic Club of Floral Park was incorporated. For the following seven years, the club met at a home on Tyson Avenue and Elizabeth Street, and by 1922, a total of 42 Masons in the Floral Park and Bellerose area signed a petition to form a lodge, which was constituted on June 8, 1923.

By 1925, an 8,500-square-foot, four-columned Greek Revival building on Tulip Avenue was erected and used primarily as a Masonic temple until 2004, when it was sold to Floral Park Village. The lodge was renamed Nassau No. 1016 from 1982 to 1995 and then changed back to Floral Park No. 1016 in late 1995. Steppingstone No. 1141 merged with Floral Park in 2008. Since 2004, Floral Park No. 1016 has been meeting in the Elks lodge on Lakeville Road in New Hyde Park. (FPL.)

The main floor of the Floral Park lodge building had a large auditorium used for local public events, with two adjoining dressing rooms. Measuring over 1,200 square feet, the room could accommodate up to 500 people with a 13-foot-wide stage that was used for recitals, speeches, and stage productions. (FPL.)

The Floral Park ladies' rest room was completely furnished by the Floral Park Chapter No. 726 of the O.E.S. The Masons used this room for entered apprentices prior to their first degree. (FPL.)

The reception room in Floral Park lodge was also used as a meeting place for Fellowcraft brothers just prior to their degrees. (FPL.)

The game room in Floral Park lodge featured two billiard tables and hand-cranked Retrola 78 rpm phonograph player. (FPL.)

The 2,300-square-foot basement banquet hall of the Floral Park lodge accommodated up to 40 people. (FPL.)

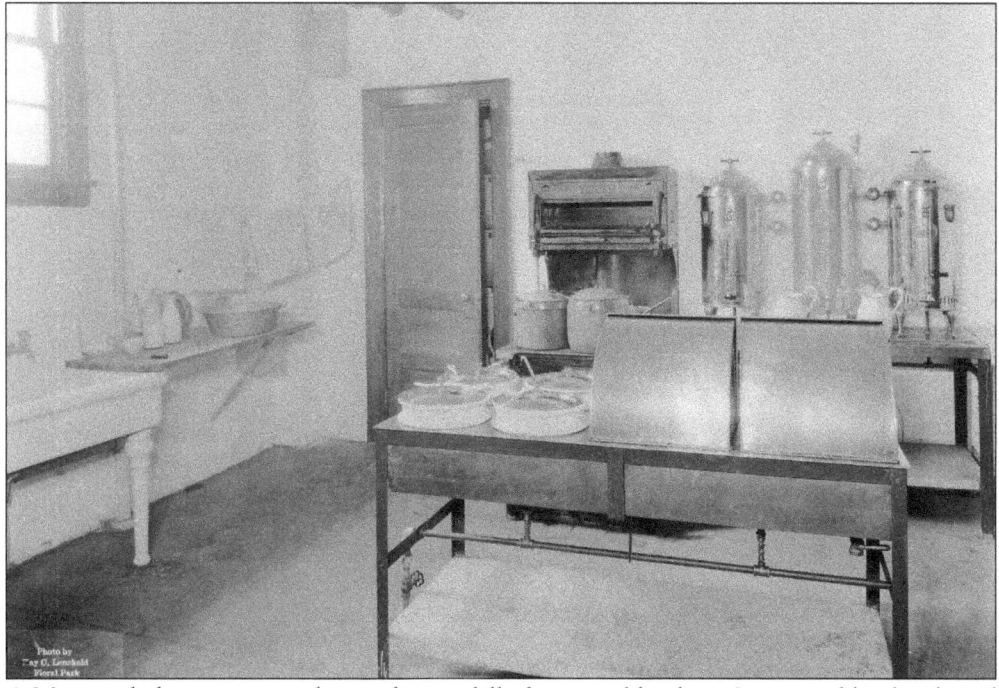

A Masonic lodge is not complete without a fully functional kitchen. Supervised by the elected junior warden and assisted by the appointed stewards, the responsible brothers prepare nourishment and refreshments for most lodge meetings and events. The Floral Park lodge kitchen was adjacent to the lower-level banquet hall (FPL.)

In 1924, the Masonic Club of Baldwin met at the home of Charles Harvey at the intersection of Grand and Milburn Avenues. Soon after, brothers from Morton No. 63, Massapequa No. 822, and Spartan No. 956 petitioned Grand Lodge of New York to form a lodge in Baldwin. The first communication of "the Friendly Lodge" was held on December 12, 1924, at the Pythias Hall on South Grand Avenue, where they met until 1939. (BHS.)

The Masonic Club of Baldwin gathers for a group picture on July 4, 1925, just six weeks after the institution of Baldwin No. 1047. The new lodge stared working closely with Sisters of Baldwin Chapter No. 779, Order of the Eastern Star, to raise funds for a new temple. Building plans continued at a fast pace through the Great Depression years, a very rare accomplishment on Long Island. The estimated cost of the building by 1939 was $30,000, made possible by the membership more than tripling in 14 years. (BHS.)

On July 8, 1939, several brothers participated in the cornerstone ceremony for Baldwin No. 1047: R∴W∴ Clifton B. Smith, district deputy grand master of the Nassau District; R∴W∴ Henry C. Turner, deputy grand master; R∴W∴ Clarence G. Glass, deputy grand marshal; R∴W∴ Harry M. Ketcham, past district deputy; R∴W∴ Robert W. Kampschulte Jr., past district deputy; R∴W∴ Archibald L. Eadie, past district deputy; W∴ Harold M. Messer, master and reverend; and R∴W∴ William R. Watson, senior grand chaplain. (RLML.)

The cornerstone laying ceremony of Baldwin lodge was one of dozens held on Long Island throughout the 20th century. One of only two public rituals, Masons have performed a special ceremony at the laying of cornerstones for new buildings since Brother George Washington officiated a similar event for the US Capitol Building in 1793. In the Masonic ceremony, the stone is checked using ancient tools, ensuring the cornerstone is square, plumb, and level, followed by consecration with corn, wine, and oil. The stone is symbolically tapped in place with a gavel at the ceremony's conclusion. (SL.)

The lodge building at 754 Prospect Street just east of Grand Avenue in Baldwin was completed by the end of 1939. Baldwin No. 1047 consolidated with Peninsula Lodge No. 1105 in 1980 and was renamed Peninsula-Baldwin No. 1047. In 1989, Peninsula-Baldwin and Oceanside No. 1140 consolidated and were renamed Prospect Lodge No. 1047. Spartan No. 956 and Prospect No. 1047 merged in 1992; the lodge is now the only building owned by a Masonic lodge in Nassau County. Wantagh-Morton No. 63 and Guiding Light–Olympia No. 808 have been meeting in Baldwin, along with several concordant Masonic organizations, for the past several years. (BHS.)

The altar and tiled mosaic floor are seen here in Baldwin lodge in 1939. The hardwood floor surrounding the mosaic section has been carpeted, but the tiles and altar are still in use today. The Masonic tradition is that the mosaic pattern of black and white stones represents the floor of the Temple of Solomon. Although Freemasonry is not a religion, the altar holds a Bible and is used for prayer. (SL.)

On May 2, 1979, Stewart Manor No. 1106 and St. Albans–Long Island No. 56 merged to form Stewart Manor–St. Albans Lodge No. 56. St. Albans No. 56 was part of the First Kings District in Brooklyn, which traces its origins to 1797. This is an image of Stewart Manor's officers in 1968. Instituted in 1929, Stewart Manor No. 1106 was part of the Second Nassau District and met primarily in Floral Park lodge. (SMSAL.)

Father and son worshipful masters of Stewart Manor No. 1106, Burt and Bill Hinchcliffe, respectively, are seen here in 1968. Today, these brothers would each wear a lewis jewel. A lewis is a tool used for lifting large objects, but in Freemasonry, it represents the son of a Freemason who joins the fraternity. Symbolically, a lewis represents a father raising his son as part of the structure of Freemasonry. A lewis jewel can be expanded to include grandfathers who were Masons. (SMSAL.)

Only three years after receiving its charter, Long Beach No. 1048 had the funds to construct a new building. The Long Beach Masonic Realty Corporation contributed equity totaling over $55,000 and a house to be used for distressed Masons, their wives, and orphans, while the new lodge members donated an additional $33,000 to Long Beach No. 1048. On October 30, 1928, hundreds gathered at 310 National Boulevard and Walnut Street in Long Beach for the cornerstone laying of the new lodge building. (SSLBL.)

Completed in early 1929 at a cost of $135,000, fundraising for the new lodge in Long Beach included mortgage bonds that were purchased by lodge members, theater performances, and a barn dance. It was owned by the Long Beach Masonic Realty Company, consisting of 21 brothers elected to annual terms. The basement featured two pool tables and four bowling alleys; the mezzanine floor had card rooms and a grill room with modern appliances. Long Beach No. 1048 surrendered its charter in 1981 and sold the building in the early 1980s. Reconstituted as Long Beach No. 1173 in 1984, the lodge met at Temple Beth El in Long Beach from 1984 to 1997 and at the Senior Citizen Community Center from 1998 to 2003. (LBL.)

Chartered in 1948, South Shore No. 1126 first met at the Odd Fellows Hall on 148 Doughty Boulevard in Inwood from 1948 to 1949. The 1911 building was designed by Marcus Christensen, a past grand brother of the International Order of Odd Fellows. The third floor is fashioned with Gothic-style windows and 18-foot ceilings, and the entire building has pressed tin cornices. Part of the First Nassau Masonic District, South Shore moved to Olympia Masonic Temple in Far Rockaway, Queens, from 1952 to 1964.

The building on the right is the Olympia Masonic Temple at 1845 Mott Avenue, Far Rockaway. Part of the Second Queens Masonic District, Olympia No. 808 rented at two different locations on Central Avenue from 1894 until erecting its own building in 1910. The Greek-style, three-story structure included four Doric 24-foot columns, a basement banquet hall, and a kitchen, while the first floor included a library and athenaeum. The second floor contained the lodge room in the rear of the building, and the third floor was a banquet room for special events. Olympia No. 808 sold the building in the 1970s.

After several years of meeting at the Olympia Masonic Temple in Far Rockaway, South Shore, No. 1126 broke ground for a new lodge building at 140 Irving Plaza, Woodmere. Pictured from left to right are M∴W∴ Harry Ostrov, grand master of Masons of New York; W∴ David Bauman, past master, South Shore; W∴ Stuart Reckseit, master; Brother Richard Estrin, president of Southshore Foundation; R∴W∴ Harry D. Koenig; and R∴W∴ Elliot Grossman. (SSLBL.)

South Shore No. 1126 met at South Shore Masonic Temple at 140 Irving Place in Woodmere from 1964 to 1993, and sold the building in 1997. South Shore No. 1126 moved to the Valley of Rockville Centre building in 1997 and merged with Long Beach No. 1173 in 2004, which was then renamed South Shore–Long Beach No. 1126, where they meet to this day. The Woodmere lodge was also the meeting place for Olympia No. 808 from 1971 to 1976. Today, the building is owned and operated by a private school. (SSLBL.)

On December 14, 1969, South Shore No. 1126, in association with United Cerebral Palsy of Nassau County, broke ground for the world's first residential care facility for the disabled with cerebral palsy at 380 Washington Avenue, Roosevelt, part of a 14-acre medical complex. Originally named the South Shore Lodge No. 1126, F.&A.M.'s Residence for Living, it contributed $100,000 for the center of orphaned cerebral palsied who could no longer be cared for by their families. Today, it is the Cerebral Palsy of Nassau County. (RLML.)

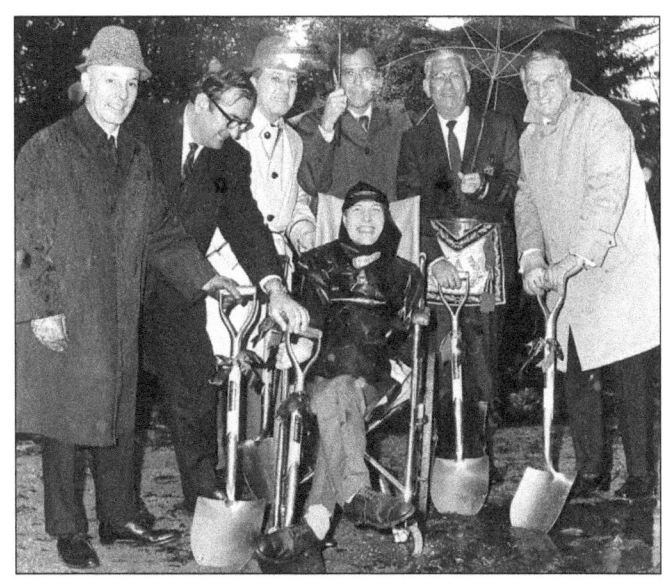

Constructed in 1926 by the Junior Order of United American Mechanics, Mechanics Hall at 30 West Jamaica Avenue in Valley Stream was home to several organizations, including the Sons of Norway, Valley Stream Flower and Garden Society, the local Republican party, Lynbrook Pythian Sisters, International Order of the Rainbow for Girls, Sherdel Paper Company, and Nassau County Police Department Fifth Precinct (1929–1963), as well as host to many weddings. Valley Stream No. 1143 began renting the second floor in 1953 and purchased the building in 1967 and remained at this location until 2005. Today, the building is owned by a Pentecostal house of worship. (NCPM.)

The officers of Guiding Light No. 1151 pose in white dinner tuxedo jackets soon after the lodge was chartered in 1955. First meeting in Rockville Centre from 1956 to 1987, in 1987, Guiding Light No. 1151 merged with Olympia No. 808 of the Second Queens District (chartered in 1894) and was renamed Guiding Light–Olympia No. 808, becoming part of the First Nassau District. In 1994, Modin No. 1153 of the First Nassau District (chartered in 1955) merged with Guiding Light–Olympia No. 808. Today, the lodge meets in the Baldwin Masonic Temple. (RLML.)

The Guiding Light Foundation endowed the Solarium at South Nassau Community Hospital in Oceanside. Established in 1965, the Guiding Light Foundation includes public service for hospitals, volunteer fire departments, and high school scholarship funds. From left to right are R∴W∴ Moses Block; Carl Pollack, secretary; Otto Stieber, first vice president; Bernard Lewis, president; Jerome Harris, second vice president; and W∴ Gerald Salk, master. (RLML.)

Six

NORTH HEMPSTEAD
WHERE THE EAST EGG AND WEST EGG MEET

Made famous by F. Scott Fitzgerald in the Roaring Twenties, the Gold Coast mansions of *The Great Gatsby* were also surrounded by Freemasonry. Occupying the Northwest corner of Nassau County, North Hempstead borders Oyster Bay in the east, Queens in the west, Hempstead in the south, and Long Island Sound in the north. Splitting off from Hempstead in 1784, North Hempstead has 30 incorporated villages, including Great Neck, Mineola, New Hyde Park, Port Washington, Roslyn, and Westbury.

North Hempstead was the last town on Long Island to see the arrival of Freemasonry. In 1906, Paumanok No. 855 started meeting in Great Neck and was the only lodge in the northwest corner of Nassau County for 15 years. The post–World War I years witnessed a thriving interest in Freemasonry in the area with Mineola No. 985 and Meadow Brook No. 1005 in 1922 and Port Washington No. 1010 in 1923, initiating over 300 new brothers in North Hempstead within a few years.

The former location of Richmond's Hardware Store in Mineola was the initial gathering place of the second North Hempstead Masonic lodge, where 49 master Masons petitioned Grand Lodge to create a new lodge. The fire house on Jericho Turnpike, later the Mineola village hall, became a regular meeting place of Mineola No. 985 when the lodge was under dispensation. In May 1922, over 800 visiting Masons gathered in the administration building of the Mineola Fair Grounds when M∴W∴ Arthur H. Tompkins, grand master of Masons in New York, presented the brethren their charter.

Soon after Paumanok No. 855 started meeting in Great Neck, dozens of brothers started work to create a new lodge in Port Washington. Ten years of challenges later, a new Masonic club with over 80 Masons was created in 1921. The club consisted of elected officers who exemplified ritual work and satisfied neighboring lodges and the Grand Lodge with their ability and integrity. First meeting in the basement of the First Methodist Episcopal Church on September 6, 1921, the Masonic Club soon moved to the local Odd Fellows Hall until Port Washington No. 1010 was chartered on June 8, 1923.

Chartered May 3, 1906, with 32 founding members, Paumanok No. 855 first met over Dodges Pharmacy in Great Neck until 1911. Located in the Robertson Building on what was Railroad Avenue, now North Station Plaza, the Victorian structure was built by Alex Robertson. The location included a general store, movie theater, and second-floor apartments; the Robertson Building gave residents and shoppers an impressive aerial view of Great Neck train station and street life. (RLML.)

Paumanok No. 855 moved to 97 North Middle Neck Road near Maple Drive in Great Neck in 1912. Dedicated in November 1911, construction was not completed until 1916. Due to rising costs of maintenance, the building was sold in the early 1960s. Paumanok No. 855 later merged with Port Washington No. 1010 and was renamed Paumanok–Port Washington No. 855.

The Paumanok No. 855 Fellowcraft Club is pictured at an outing at Karatsonis in Glenwood, New York, on August 11, 1920. Karatsonis included a hotel, park grounds, and a pavilion near Sea Cliff. A Fellowcraft club, also known as a Square club, is either a subset of a Masonic lodge or revolves around a specific profession. The club is where Masons hold gatherings, including barbeques, where there is a more casual and friendly environment without any of the ritual found in a regular lodge meeting.

Port Washington No. 1010 was chartered on June 8, 1923, with most of the petitioners from Paumanok No. 355 in Great Neck. The lodge met at the Odd Fellows Hall on South Washington Street until October 1927, when it moved to Columbia Hall on Locust Street. In May 1925, the lodge purchased a site on Middle Neck Road for $11,000. Fundraising began for a property on Middle Neck Road, some of which was channeled through the "Port Pranks" Musical Revues in the mid-1930s. The building was dedicated in 1940, a short walk from the Port Washington train station.

Chartered May 15, 1922, Mineola No. 985 first met at the fire house on Jericho Turnpike, later the site of the village hall. Equipment for the lodge was contracted and paid for by a $10 assessment on each signer of the original petition. The lodge later rented space at the Odd Fellows Temple on 236 Willis Avenue, Mineola, from 1929 to 2009. Garden City No. 1083 briefly met here in 1973, and New Hyde Park No. 1160 rented the lodge from 1972 to 1977. (MHS.)

The Odd Fellows building is seen here as it appeared in the 1950s, with signs advertising the IOOF, Mineola Masonic Lodge, and Nassau Baptist Church. Sold in 2009, Mineola Lodge moved to 18 West Nicolai Street in Hicksville and later consolidated with Bethpage-Hicksville No. 975. The building is currently owned by the First Korean Church of New York. (MHS.)

Pictured are two examples of the different outfits a Masonic brother sometimes wears in a tiled meeting. Both pictures of Mineola Lodge were taken in the west of the fire house lodge room on Jericho Turnpike in the mid-1920s. Above, several of the officers are in formal wear for a stated communication, which occurs at least once a month. Below are most of the same brothers, now dressed for the Mineola Degree Team as several different characters in the third-degree drama on the building of King Solomon's temple. Brothers who are appointed or elected officers of a lodge are required to wear tuxedos, while visiting brethren not holding an office position may come to meetings wearing business attire. (Both, MHS.)

The Williston Masonic Club was organized in 1927, and by 1962, over 100 lodges were represented in the organization. The club owned a building at 700 Willis Avenue in Williston Park for decades, hosting a variety of events, including fellowcraft clubs and warden associations, and managing its own degree team. For over 30 years, the Williston Masonic Club and Mineola No. 985 co-sponsored an annual church service and breakfast at East Williston Community Church. Later the site of Riverbay Restaurant, the property was sold to a bank in 2013.

Chartered May 3, 1922, Hollis No. 922 originated among the members of the Hollis Auxiliary of the American Red Cross just prior to US involvement in World War I. The lodge met in this building on 191st Street, between Jamaica and Woodhull Avenues, Hollis, Queens, from 1924 to 1975, when it moved to the Kismet Shrine in Hicksville. In 1997, Hollis Lodge moved to the Second Nassau Masonic District, and today, it is part of Bethpage-Hicksville No. 975.

On March 31, 1921, thirty-eight master Masons residing in Westbury and its vicinity met to discuss the forming of a lodge. Chartered on May 7, 1923, Meadow Brook Lodge No. 1005 originally met at Winthrop Hall of the Episcopal Church of the Advent from 1922 to 1926. Meadow Brook No. 1005 purchased a lot at 240 Maple Avenue in Westbury and met at this location from December 14, 1926, to December 11, 1979.

The Meadow Brook lodge building was sold on January 4, 1980, and its members started meeting at the Hicksville Masonic Lodge, later going through several mergers. It is now part of the history of Bethpage-Hicksville No. 975. Today, the building is an annex to the Ava Maria Catholic Church in Westbury. (WMPL.)

Constituted on June 3, 1926, Sunrise No. 1069 was the second Masonic lodge in Freeport, with 217 charter members residing in Nassau and Suffolk Counties, averaging 70 percent meeting attendance for the first several years. After meeting for almost 30 years in Spartan Lodge in Freeport, Sunrise purchased a plot of land at 286 West Merrick Road, Freeport, to construct a Lodge building. This photograph was taken in 1957 prior to the construction of the Sunrise Masonic Lodge. (SL.)

Dedicated on November 14, 1957, Sunrise met in its own building for the next 20 years. Sunrise consolidated with Laurelton No. 1131 in 1979, and the new lodge was named Sunrise-Laurelton No. 1069. Sunrise-Laurelton No. 1069 merged with Spartan No. 956 in 2003. This building is now owned by the Tabernacle of Faith. (RLML.)

R∴W∴ Sidney Burns donated funds from the newly created Sunrise Laurelton Masonic Lodge Endowed Scholarship to the president of Hofstra University, James M. Shuart, in August 1984. Led by W∴ Richard G. Fromwick and foundation chairman W∴ Edwin H. Dembicer, Sunrise-Laurelton also started a fundraising project for the South Nassau Community Hospital in Oceanside. (SL.)

In 1952, the Great Neck Square Club approached Paumanok No. 855 to start the process of forming a lodge. Steppingstone No. 1141 received its dispensation on May 18, 1953, with 400 brothers present and over 200 additional brothers turned away due to overcrowding. Steppingstone No. 1141 met in the Elks lodge and a synagogue in Great Neck before merging with Floral Park No. 1016 in 2008. (RLML.)

A group of master Masons from the Laurelton Square Club petitioned Grand Lodge to form a Masonic lodge in Queens. By June 1950, Laurelton No. 1131 was constituted and was part of the Second Queens Masonic District. Pictured is the first line of officers, with W∴ Marx I. Murzin seated at center. The lodge met at Springfield Gardens No. 1057 from 1950 to 1968 before moving to the Bellmore Masonic Temple on Bedford Avenue and Square Place from 1969 to 1978.

Laurelton No. 1131 consolidated with Sunrise No. 1069 in 1979 and was renamed Sunrise-Laurelton No. 1069. This lodge merged with South Bay No. 1145 in 2003 and finally with Spartan No. 956 in 2014. Pictured is the Springfield Masonic Lodge at 138–135 Springfield Boulevard, Springfield Gardens, Queens, where Laurelton No. 1131 met from 1950 to 1968. The 1925 building is now home to the Agape Church of God. (SL.)

Seven

GLEN COVE
A LONG ISLAND CITY

In 1917, Glen Cove became an independent city, breaking off from the Town of Oyster Bay 250 years after initially becoming a part of its jurisdiction. Prior to 1866, the area comprising the present Nassau County was under the jurisdiction of Morton No. 63 of Hempstead. Brothers wishing to travel to lodge meetings had to go by horse or foot, a difficult journey of several miles for most brothers residing on the north shore of Long Island.

In 1864, Freemasons in the Glen Cove area petitioned Morton No. 63 for dispensation to form a lodge. Concerned with losing members, Morton No. 63's master rejected the petition, forcing the Glen Cove brothers to try again the following year when a new master was elected. On March 10, 1866, a total of 11 Glen Cove–area brothers received a dispensation to institute a lodge. Not all the founding members were members of Morton No. 63, but were brothers raised as master Masons during the Civil War. Most of the new Glen Cove brothers were connected to the local Duryea Starch Factory, one of the world's leading manufacturers of starch, owned by Gen. Hiram Duryea and his brother Col. George Duryea, organizers of the infamous Civil War Duryea Zouaves.

The name for Glen Cove No. 580 was chosen from a list selected by an appointed committee, including Giblam, Triumph, Minnehaha, and Ionic. The new lodge first rented rooms from the local Odd Fellows in Pembroke Hall on School Street. Rental of $1.50 per evening included light and heat, and members were charged $3 annual dues.

The antagonism with the Hempstead lodge over jurisdiction disputes continued in 1867, when the new master of Morton No. 63 was convinced that his lodge covered a wider area east to west, bounded by Long Island Sound on the north and the Atlantic Ocean on the south, with complaints of "poaching" members from each lodge proving to be accurate. The disputes were settled after months of negotiations between the lodges.

Members of Glen Cove No. 580 went on to form several lodges on Long Island, including Matinecock No. 806, Paumanok No. 855, Bethpage No. 975, Mineola No. 985, Meadow Brook No. 1005, Port Washington No. 1010, and Manetto No. 1025.

Chartered in 1866, Glen Cove No. 580 was originally named Ionic Lodge but changed to Glen Cove when it was discovered there was already a lodge named Ionic No. 110. The lodge first rented rooms in the Odd Fellows Hall, also known as Pembroke Hall, on School Street, Glen Cove, for $1.50 per night. Over the next 30 years, Glen Cove met in several locations, including buildings owned by Brother George Wilcoxsen from 1869 to 1873 and Benjamin Kirk from 1873 to 1895 before leasing the top floor of the new Glen Cove Mutual Insurance Company on Glen Street from 1895 to 1913. In 1995, two adjacent buildings were joined together with the three-story structure, which now serves as the Glen Cove city hall.

Several of the Duryea brothers were Masons from Glen Cove No 580 and members of the famous Duryea Zouaves. Led by Gen. Abram Duryée, the 5th New York Volunteer Infantry was a regiment of the Union army stationed in Fort Schuyler in Throgs Neck and was best known for modeling its tactics and uniforms after the French Zouaves of the Crimean War. The uniforms were dark blue Zouave jackets with red trim, dark blue shirt with red trim, a red Zouave sash with sky blue trim and baggy red pantaloons, red fez with yellow tassel, white gaiters, and leather leggings. The regiment is pictured at the Fort Schuyler adjutant mess on May 18, 1861. The regiment fought several battles, including the Battle of Gaines' Mill of the Seven Days Battles, repelling a Confederate counterattack against Brig. Gen. Maxcy Gregg's South Carolina brigade. The 5th suffered its greatest loss at the Second Battle of Bull Run when 120 Zouaves were killed within eight minutes; it was the greatest single battle fatality of all Federal volunteer infantry regiments in the Civil War. (PD.)

In 1909, Glen Cove No. 580 purchased a building on Continental Avenue originally constructed by Brother Edgar Duryea of the Duryea Zouaves and held its first meeting on February 5, 1913. Under the suggestion of W∴ William H. Lang, $12,000 in bonds were sold to the membership, thus retaining ownership with the Glen Cove brothers. Approximately two thirds of the bonds were later sold by Lang, who rode door to door on his bicycle. The lodge met in this building for the last time on February 14, 1973, just prior to vacating for the new owners, Dymer Communications Corporation. (ML.)

This is a rare example of lodge officers sitting as a group for their official portrait. Glen Cove Lodge's 1925 officers are, from left to right, (first row) Carl Phillips, tiler; and John Manafort, secretary; (second row) Seymour Warrant, treasurer; Frank J. Vernon, steward; Edwin C. Braynard, junior deacon; Thomas J. Watkins, senior warden; Mortimer H. Rudyard, master; Arthur Arthurhead, junior warden; Chris O'Levin, senior master of ceremonies; Andrew Holback, junior master of ceremonies; and George Raymond, chaplain. (GCL.)

This one-of-a-kind artifact is a large cast iron fire bell. Forged in honor of W∴ Frank Wechtel, master of Glen Cove No. 580 in 1958, the piece was dedicated on May 10, 1973, in honor of the longtime member. Weighing close to 100 pounds and measuring over two feet high, the bell is currently on display in the Matinecock Masonic Museum in Oyster Bay. (GCL.)

In January 1974, Glen Cove No. 580 purchased a building at 240 Glen Avenue, Sea Cliff, from the James F. Brengel post of the American Legion. Constructed in 1891, the building at one time was the parish house for St. Luke's Episcopal Church and today is a single-family residence. (RLML.)

Townsend Scudder was a member of Glen Cove No. 580 and the grand master of Masons in New York from 1906 to 1907, becoming the first brother from Nassau or Suffolk Counties to be elected most worshipful. Raised a master Mason in 1889, he was Glen Cove's master from 1891 to 1892; district deputy of the First Masonic District from 1892 to 1894; senior grand deacon from 1894 to 1895; commissioner of appeals from 1895 to 1903; deputy grand master from 1904 to 1906 and trustee of the Masonic Hall and Asylum Fund. The Northport native was a Democratic congressman, justice of the New York Supreme Court (second district), state park commissioner, and vice president of the Long Island State Park Commission under Pres. Robert Moses. In 1927, Scudder was appointed to the New York Supreme Court by Gov. Alfred E. Smith and was supported by both political parties for the next 14 years, retiring from the bench at the age of 70. An avid dog lover, he was the best in show judge at the Westminster Kennel Club dog show in 1932. (LOC.)

Eight

Concordant Bodies
Further Light in Masonry

There is no degree higher or more important in Freemasonry than that of master Mason. Yet, Freemasonry does not end upon being raised a master Mason, and it is not closed off to women or young adults. Several affiliated bodies and youth organizations have remained popular throughout North America and the world. The more recognizable groups include the Shriners, Eastern Star, and the Scottish Rite, but there are several other concordant bodies that outsiders of the fraternity may not be familiar with.

The additional Masonic degrees are supervised by separate grand bodies and open to master Masons in good standing. The two principal concordant bodies are the Ancient and Accepted Scottish Rite and the York Rite. The Scottish Rite consists of the fourth through 32nd degrees, a series of morality lessons that continue a master Mason's education in many ways. Recipients of the 33rd degree are elected by a supreme council from members who have made major contributions to society and Freemasonry.

The York Rite has three separate bodies: the Royal Arch Chapter, the Council of Royal and Select Masters (Cryptic Masonry), and Commandery of the Knights Templar. According to legend, the first meetings of Masons took place in the ancient city of York in northern England, a name later adopted by Masons for a series of progressive degrees of the York Rite. The first stage of the Royal Arch consists of four additional degrees, an extension of the three degrees of a master Mason lodge. The Cryptic degrees are the second and final part that deal specifically with the Hiramic legend of the master Mason degrees. The Knights Templar is the final order of the York Rite, open only to Christian Masons, founded on the unverified theories that after the persecution of the Knights Templar in 1312, the disbanded organization took refuge in Freemasonry.

Other affiliated bodies include the Tall Cedars of Lebanon, a group organized in symbolic forests with members wearing a pyramid-shaped hat. The Royal Order of Jesters is an exclusive invitation-only court offered to 13 members in good standing of the shrine. The Order of the Amaranth is open to master Masons and their female relatives. A branch of the fraternity founded for African Americans in 1784 is Prince Hall Freemasonry, named after its founder, abolitionist Prince Hall of Boston. Several Prince Hall lodges continue to meet on Long Island today and are recognized by the Grand Lodge of New York.

Kismet Shriners are seen at a charity golf outing in the 1920s. Founded in 1870, the Shriners created the first Shriners Hospital for Children in 1922 to combat polio. Each member was originally charged $2 to fund the construction of the first hospital. Today, there is a network of 22 Shriner hospitals in North America, each offering free care for children without insurance and waiving all out-of-pocket costs, treating orthopedic injuries, disease, burns, spinal cord injuries, and birth defects, including cleft lip and palate. (JL.)

The Kismet Shriners march in a New York City parade in the 1930s. One of the most recognizable aspects of Freemasonry, yet the one least connected to the fraternity, are Shriners marching in parades. Proudly wearing fezzes and sometimes squeezing into little cars, the Ancient Arabic Order of the Nobles of the Mystic Shrine focuses more on fun and fellowship than the other bodies of organized rituals. (KS.)

Uniformed members of the Kismet Shrine are pictured at the Tomb of the Unknown Soldier in Arlington National Cemetery, Virginia, on June 13, 1935. In 1887, Noble Wayland Trask organized Kismet Temple in Brooklyn. First meeting at 38 Court Street, Kismet Temple soon moved to the Aurora Grata Cathedral at Bedford and Madison Avenues, where it remained until 1910. (KS.)

The oldest surviving Shrine mosque in America was built in 1910 at 92 Herkimer Street, Bedford Stuyvesant, Brooklyn. The auditorium seated over 2,300, and the banquet hall held over 1,000 and was designed, planned, and supervised by architect Richard Thomas Short, a Kismet noble. In 1932 it was a movie theater, and throughout the 1930s, band concerts were performed there on Sundays. Sold to a Baptist church in 1966 for $250,000, the building still retains its original Shriner markings and is listed in the National Register of Historic Places. Kismet Shrine moved to Hicksville, where it continues to meet. (KS.)

The Jephthah Daughters Order of the Eastern Star are pictured at Jephtha Lodge in Huntington in 1931. The Order of the Eastern Star is a Masonic appendant group open to both men and women. Founded in 1850 by attorney and educator Rob Morris, the order was not approved as an appendant body of Freemasonry until 1873. Members must be 18 years or older, and men must be master Masons. Originally open only to daughters, wives, sisters, mothers, and widows of Masons, the order now accepts other members outside the fraternity. (HHS.)

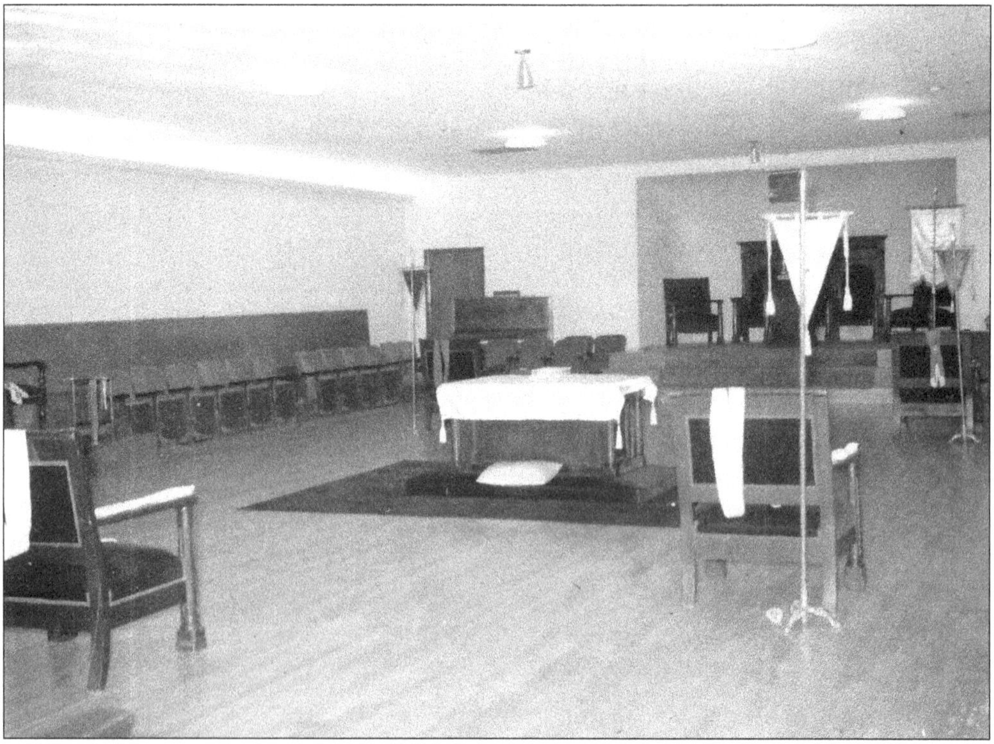

The Smithtown lodge room is set up for a meeting of the Order of the Eastern Star in 1960. The emblem of the order is a five-pointed star, with the letters FATAL surrounding the center pentagon, representing "Fairest Among Thousands, Altogether Lovely." The order's lessons are stories inspired by Biblical figures, including Adah, Ruth, Esther, Martha, and Electa. There are 18 elected and appointed officers in a chapter, led by a worthy matron and a worthy patron, a master Mason who provides general support. (SML.)

Melchizedek Chapter No. 273, Royal Arch Chapter, is pictured in Glen Cove Lodge. Royal Arch Masonry is the first of three parts of the York Rite, a series of progressive degrees after a brother is raised to the third degree of Masonry. The rite's name is derived from the city of York, England, where, according to Masonic legend, the first meetings of English Masons took place in the early 18th century. Royal Arch Masons meet as a chapter instead of a lodge, and the members are referred to as companions instead of brothers. The four degrees of a chapter are mark master Mason, past master, most excellent master, and royal arch mason, and until the end of the 18th century, Royal Arch rituals were part of the master Mason lodge. The first lodge on Long Island, Huntington No. 26, was part of the York Rite Grand Lodge. The second and third bodies of the York Rite are the Council of Royal and Select Masters (also known as the Council of Cryptic Masons) and the Commandery of Knights Templar. Each York Rite organization is governed independently. (GCL.)

Nassau Commandery No. 73, Knights Templar met in Hempstead for many years before moving to Oyster Bay. The Knights Templar require a belief in the Christian faith, unlike most of the other Masonic orders, in which membership only requires belief in a supreme being regardless of religious affiliation. A Knights Templar commandery is the final body of the York Rite, a series of progressive degrees after master Mason. Before joining the Templar, a companion needs to progress through a chapter of the Royal Arch Masons and a Council of Royal and Select Masters. (NCPA.)

Patchogue Commandery No. 65 in the Meridian Masonic Lodge, Islip, is seen here on May 4, 1964. Chartered September 5, 1900, Patchogue is the oldest active commandery on Long Island; it and Nassau No. 73 are the only active Knights Templar commanderies meeting in the Suffolk and Nassau Districts today. Huntington Commandery No. 70 was constituted on September 18, 1914, and met in Jephtha Lodge in Huntington before dissolving in the 1970s. (RLML.)

Pictured is the Long Island Council of Princes of Jerusalem, representing the 16th degree of the Scottish Rite. The Valley of Rockville Centre is a member of the Supreme Council of the Ancient Accepted Scottish Rite of the Northern Masonic Jurisdiction. The Scottish Rite is an extension of the Freemasonry degrees, building upon the ethical philosophy offered in the first three degrees of a master Mason lodge. Degrees four through thirty-two are each portrayed through dramatic presentations. The 33rd degree is an honorary member of the Supreme Council. (VRC.)

Seen here is the Long Island Chapter of Rose Croix before the presentation of the 18th degree, in the Valley of Rockville Centre. After reaching the third degree of master Mason, a brother can join the Scottish Rite, whereby an additional 29 degrees are presented, which can take several years to complete. The 33rd degree is an honor for service to society and the fraternity and is awarded to a small select group every two years. The additional degrees do not give a brother a higher rank in Masonry, but a parallel series of Masonic lessons. (VRC.)

The first members of the Southampton Chapter of the DeMolay at Old Town No. 908, Southampton, are pictured here in 1947. Founded in 1919 as a youth-driven nonprofit for young men aged 12 to 21, the DeMolay assists the community, fostering connections and building leadership skills. Founded in Kansas City, Missouri, the organization is named after Jacques de Molay, the last grand master of the Knights Templar. (OTL.)

This image was captured during the installation of officers of Truth Triangle No. 31 on November 11, 1966, in Jephtha Lodge, Huntington. Active for over 90 years in New York, the Organization of Triangles is one of two youth organizations for young ladies between the ages of 10 and 21. The other is the International Order of Rainbow for Girls. The character building, service-oriented sisterhood builds a foundation for its members to develop the life skills of leadership, citizenship, public speaking, teamwork, confidence, and self-esteem. (TT.)

Masonic Suffolk Post War Vets, Post No. 23, is pictured at Babylon Lodge. Chartered in 1948 as a unit of the Grand Lodge of New York, the post consists of Masonic war veterans, carrying our nation's colors for official events, parades, and other community activities. The Suffolk post was chartered on October 23, 1952. Masonic Brothers who were regularly enlisted, drafted, inducted, or commissioned in the Navy, Army, Coast Guard, Marine Corps, Air Force, Merchant Marine, or any federal armed force that is accorded veteran status with an honorable discharge is eligible to join. (BL.)

Past presidents of the Long Island Railroad Square Club are seen here in 1937. A square club was originally formed in the 1920s centering around occupations, trades, or civil service and introduced Masons from other lodges who shared the same occupation. Part of the National League of Masonic Clubs, there have been a variety of square clubs throughout Long Island, including police, fire, post office, electricians, printers, pharmaceutical, textiles, Grumman aircraft, and even a digital square club for web-related professionals. (BL.)

Visit us at
arcadiapublishing.com

www.ingramcontent.com/pod-product-compliance
Lightning Source LLC
Chambersburg PA
CBHW060936170426
43194CB00027B/2976